Good Housekeeping
Easy autumn
food

Good Housekeeping
Easy autumn food

COLLINS & BROWN

NOTES

- Both metric and imperial measures are given for the recipes. Follow either set of measures, not a mixture of both, as they are not interchangeable.
- All spoon measures are level.
  1 tsp = 5ml spoon; 1 tbsp = 15ml spoon.
- Ovens and grills must be preheated to the specified temperature.
- Use sea salt and freshly ground black pepper unless otherwise suggested.
- Fresh herbs should be used unless dried herbs are specified in a recipe.
- Medium eggs should be used except where otherwise specified. Free-range eggs are recommended.
- Note that certain recipes, including mayonnaise, lemon curd and some cold desserts, contain raw or lightly cooked eggs. The young, elderly, pregnant women and anyone with an immune-deficiency disease should avoid these, because of the slight risk of salmonella.
- Calorie counts per serving are provided for the recipes.

Contents

Foreword

I love the changing of the seasons and nothing excites me more than the time when summer turns slowly into autumn. The trees gradually change from fresh greens to rich, golden-coloured hues and you begin to feel a cooler chill in the air. There's a wealth of gorgeous produce in the shops, too. Orchard fruits and earthy vegetables which take longer to cook all come into their own. The fresh light summer recipes, that can be whipped up in no time, make way for richer more hearty dishes which are still just as easy to put together as this book shows.

Getting supper on the table has never been easier or simpler. Whether you fancy something light and quick, such as my favourite sticky chicken thighs, or slow and long, like the lamb and leek hotpot, you'll find it all here. And if you fancy something sweet, take your pick from the puddings chapter. Oranges with caramel sauce anyone? All the recipes have been triple tested in the Good Housekeeping Institute so, when you come to make them, they'll look and taste just as delicious, too.

Emma

Emma Marsden

Cookery Editor

Good Housekeeping

Soups and Starters

Freezing Tip

Cool the soup at the end of step 2, then freeze for up to one month.
To use Thaw overnight in the refrigerator. Reheat gently and simmer for 5 minutes. Stir in the freshly chopped coriander.

Carrot and Sweet Potato Soup

1 tbsp olive oil

1 large onion, chopped

1 tbsp coriander seeds

900g (2lb) carrots, roughly chopped

2 medium sweet potatoes, roughly chopped

2 litres (3½ pints) hot vegetable or chicken stock

2 tbsp white wine vinegar

2 tbsp freshly chopped coriander, plus extra fresh sprigs to garnish

8 tbsp half-fat crème fraîche

salt and ground black pepper

1 Heat the oil in a large pan, add the onion and coriander seeds and cook over a medium heat for 5 minutes. Add the carrots and sweet potatoes and cook for a further 5 minutes.

2 Add the stock and bring the soup to the boil. Reduce the heat and leave to simmer for 25 minutes. Cool slightly, then put in a blender and whiz until slightly chunky. Add the vinegar and season with salt and pepper.

3 Pour the soup into a clean pan, stir in the chopped coriander and reheat gently.

4 Divide the soup among eight warmed bowls, then garnish each with 1 tbsp crème fraîche and fresh coriander sprigs to serve.

Preparation Time: 15 minutes

Cooking Time: 45 minutes

Serves: 8

Calories Per Serving: 120

Try Something Different

Try this with sausages instead of the chicken.
Italian Marinade Mix 1 crushed garlic clove with
4 tbsp olive oil, the juice of 1 lemon and 1 tsp
dried oregano. If you like, leave to marinate for
1–2 hours before cooking.
Oriental Marinade Mix together 2 tbsp soy sauce,
1 tsp demerara sugar, 2 tbsp dry sherry or apple
juice, 1 tsp finely chopped fresh root ginger and
1 crushed garlic clove.
Honey and Mustard Mix together 2 tbsp grain
mustard, 3 tbsp clear honey and the grated zest
and juice of 1 lemon.

Sticky Chicken Thighs

1 Preheat the oven to 200°C (180°C fan oven)
mark 6. Put the garlic into a bowl with the
honey and chilli sauce, and mix together.
Add the chicken thighs and toss to coat.

2 Put into a roasting tin and roast for
15–20 minutes until the chicken is golden
and cooked through. Serve with rice and
a crisp green salad.

1 garlic clove, crushed

1 tbsp clear honey

1 tbsp Thai sweet chilli sauce

4 chicken thighs

rice and green salad to serve

Preparation Time: 5 minutes

Cooking Time: 15–20 minutes

Serves: 4

Calories Per Serving: 218

Try Something Different

Replace the smoked tofu with shredded leftover roast chicken and simmer for 2–3 minutes.

Full-of-goodness Broth

1–2 tbsp medium curry paste

200ml (7fl oz) reduced-fat coconut milk

600ml (1 pint) hot vegetable stock

200g (7oz) smoked tofu, cubed

2 pak choi, chopped

a handful of sugarsnap peas

4 spring onions, chopped

lime to serve

1   Heat the curry paste in a pan for 1–2 minutes. Add the coconut milk and hot vegetable stock.

2   Bring to the boil, then add the smoked tofu, pak choi, sugarsnap peas and spring onions. Simmer for 1–2 minutes. Divide among four bowls and serve with a squeeze of lime.

Preparation Time: 10 minutes

Cooking Time: 6–8 minutes

Serves: 6

Calories Per Serving: 106

American Sticky Ribs

900g (2lb) lean pork spare ribs

125g (4oz) hoisin sauce

2 tbsp mild clear honey

2 tsp English mustard

3 tsp white wine or cider vinegar

4 tbsp tomato ketchup

2 garlic cloves, crushed

4 tbsp fresh apple or orange juice

coleslaw, onion rings and orange wedges to serve

1 Preheat the oven to 200°C (180°C fan oven) mark 6. Line a large tin with a double layer of foil and spread the ribs over the base.

2 Whisk together the remaining ingredients in a bowl, then spoon over the pork – it may look as though there isn't enough liquid but the ribs will release plenty of juices as they cook.

3 Cover with foil and cook for 20 minutes. Turn the ribs over, then put back in the oven, uncovered. Cook for 40–45 minutes, basting occasionally, until they are dark golden and sticky, and most of the liquid has gone. Serve hot, with coleslaw, onion rings and orange wedges.

Preparation Time: 10 minutes

Cooking Time: about 1 hour

Serves: 4

Calories Per Serving: 485

Cook's Tip

Chillies vary enormously in strength, from quite mild to blisteringly hot, depending on the type of chilli and its ripeness. Taste a small piece first to check it's not too hot for you.

Be extremely careful when handling chillies not to touch or rub your eyes with your fingers, as the chilli juices will sting. Wash knives immediately after handling chillies for the same reason. As a precaution, use rubber gloves when preparing them if you like.

Chicken and Bean Soup

1 tbsp olive oil

1 onion, finely chopped

4 celery sticks, chopped

1 red chilli, seeded and roughly chopped (see Cook's Tip)

2 skinless chicken breasts, cut into strips

1 litre (1¾ pints) hot chicken or vegetable stock

100g (3½oz) bulgur wheat

2 x 400g cans cannellini beans, drained

400g can chopped tomatoes

25g (1oz) flat-leafed parsley, roughly chopped

wholegrain bread and hummus to serve

1 Heat the oil in a large, heavy-based pan. Add the onion, celery and chilli, and cook over a low heat for 10 minutes or until softened. Add the chicken and stir-fry for 3–4 minutes until golden.

2 Add the stock to the pan and bring to a simmer. Stir in the bulgur wheat and simmer for 15 minutes. Stir in the cannellini beans and tomatoes, and return to a simmer. Ladle into bowls and sprinkle with the chopped parsley. Serve with wholegrain bread and hummus.

Preparation Time: 10 minutes

Cooking Time: 30 minutes

Serves: 4

Calories Per Serving: 351

Cook's Tip

Kabocha is a Japanese variety of winter squash, and has a dull-coloured deep green skin with whitish stripes. Its flesh is an intense yellow-orange colour.

900g (2lb) pumpkin or squash, such as butternut, crown prince or kabocha (see Cook's Tip), peeled, seeded and chopped into roughly 2cm (3/4 in) cubes

1 garlic clove, crushed

2 tbsp olive oil

2 x 400g cans chickpeas, drained

1/2 red onion, thinly sliced

1 large bunch coriander, roughly chopped

salt and ground black pepper

steamed spinach to serve

For the tahini sauce

1 large garlic clove, crushed

3 tbsp tahini paste

juice of 1 lemon

Pumpkin with Chickpeas

1 Preheat the oven to 220°C (200°C fan oven) mark 7. Toss the squash or pumpkin with the garlic and oil, and season. Put in a roasting tin and roast for 25 minutes or until soft.

2 Meanwhile, put the chickpeas in a pan with 150ml (1/4 pint) water over a medium heat, to warm through.

3 To make the tahini sauce, put the garlic in a bowl, add a pinch of salt, then whisk in the tahini paste. Add the lemon juice and 4–5 tbsp cold water – enough to make a consistency somewhere between single and double cream – and season.

4 Drain the chickpeas, put in a large bowl, then add the pumpkin, onion and coriander. Pour on the tahini sauce and toss carefully. Adjust the seasoning and serve while warm, with spinach.

Preparation Time: 15 minutes

Cooking Time: 25–30 minutes

Serves: 6

Calories Per Serving: 228

Warm Lentil and Egg Salad

1 tbsp olive oil

1 onion, 1 carrot and 1 celery stick, finely chopped

2 red peppers, seeded and roughly chopped

200g (7oz) flat mushrooms, sliced

200g (7oz) lentils, rinsed and drained

600ml (1 pint) hot vegetable stock

4 medium eggs

100g (3½ oz) baby leaf spinach

2 tbsp balsamic vinegar

ground black pepper

1   Heat the oil in a large pan. Add the onion, carrot and celery, and cook for 5 minutes. Add the peppers and mushrooms. Cover and cook for a further 5 minutes. Stir in the lentils and stock. Bring to the boil and simmer, covered, for 25–30 minutes.

2   Meanwhile, bring a large pan of water to the boil. Break the eggs into the water and cook for 3–4 minutes. Lift them out with a slotted spoon, drain on kitchen paper and keep warm.

3   A couple of minutes before the end of the lentil cooking time, add the spinach and cook until wilted. Stir in the vinegar. Spoon on to four plates or bowls and top each with a poached egg. Season with pepper and serve.

Preparation Time: 15 minutes

Cooking Time: 35–40 minutes

Serves: 4

Calories Per Serving: 317

Easy Pea Soup

1 small baguette, thinly sliced

2 tbsp basil-infused olive oil, plus extra to drizzle

450g (1lb) frozen peas, thawed

600ml (1 pint) vegetable stock

salt and ground black pepper

1 Preheat the oven to 220°C (200°C fan oven) mark 7. To make the croûtons, put the bread on a baking sheet, drizzle with 2 tbsp oil and bake for 10–15 minutes until golden.

2 Meanwhile, put the peas in a food processor, add the stock and season with salt and pepper. Whiz for 2–3 minutes.

3 Pour the soup into a pan and bring to the boil, then reduce the heat and simmer for 10 minutes. Spoon into warmed bowls, add the croûtons, drizzle with extra oil and sprinkle with salt and pepper. Serve immediately.

Preparation Time: 2 minutes, plus thawing

Cooking Time: 15 minutes

Serves: 4

Calories Per Serving: 408

Leek and Potato Soup

25g (1oz) butter

1 onion, finely chopped

1 garlic clove, crushed

550g (1¼lb) leeks, chopped

200g (7oz) floury potatoes, peeled and sliced

1.3 litres (2¼ pints) hot vegetable stock

crème fraîche and chopped chives to garnish

1 Melt the butter in a pan over a gentle heat, add the onion and cook for 10–15 minutes until soft. Add the garlic and cook for a further 1 minute. Add the leeks and cook for 5–10 minutes until softened. Add the potatoes and toss together with the leeks.

2 Pour in the hot stock and bring to the boil. Simmer the soup for 20 minutes until the potatoes are tender. Cool a little, then purée in a food processor.

3 Reheat before serving, garnished with crème fraîche and chives.

Preparation Time: 10 minutes

Cooking Time: 40–45 minutes

Serves: 4

Calories Per Serving: 117

Cook's Tip

If your fishcakes tend to fall apart, put them in the refrigerator for about 2 hours (or 30 minutes in the freezer) before cooking them.

900g (2lb) floury potatoes, such as Maris Piper, peeled and quartered

900g (2lb) salmon fillets

juice of 1 lemon

4 tbsp mayonnaise

pinch of cayenne pepper

2 tbsp freshly chopped herbs, such as tarragon, basil or parsley

2 tbsp chilli oil

salt and ground black pepper

lemon wedges to garnish

green salad to serve

Herby Lemon Fishcakes

1 Put the potatoes in a large pan of cold salted water, cover and bring to the boil. Turn down the heat and simmer for about 20 minutes or until tender. Drain well, put the pan back on the heat to dry the potatoes, then mash.

2 Put the salmon in a pan with 600ml (1 pint) cold water and half the lemon juice. Cover and bring to the boil, then simmer for 1 minute. Turn off the heat and leave to cool in the water for 20–30 minutes.

3 Preheat the oven to 200°C (180°C fan oven) mark 6. Drain the fish, remove the skin and discard, then flake the fish. Add to the potato along with the remaining lemon juice, the mayonnaise, cayenne pepper and chopped herbs. Season and mix together.

4 Line a large baking sheet with foil. Put a 7.5cm (3in) plain cooking ring on the baking sheet and fill with some of the mixture. Lift off, then repeat with the remainder of the mixture to make eight cakes. Drizzle with chilli oil and cook for 25 minutes or until golden. Garnish with lemon wedges and serve with a green salad.

Preparation Time: 25 minutes, plus cooling

Cooking Time: 45 minutes

Serves: 4

Calories Per Serving: 721

Roast Mushrooms with Pesto

8 portobello mushrooms

8 tbsp fresh pesto

toasted ciabatta, salad and basil leaves to serve

1 Preheat the oven to 200°C (180°C fan oven) mark 6. Put the mushrooms into an ovenproof dish, then spoon 1 tbsp fresh pesto on top of each one.

2 Pour 150ml (¼ pint) boiling water into the tin, then cook for 15 minutes until the mushrooms are soft and the topping is hot. Serve with toasted ciabatta and salad, and scatter a few small basil leaves over.

Preparation Time: 5 minutes

Cooking Time: 15 minutes

Serves: 4

Calories Per Serving: 258

Try Something Different

To give the soup more of a kick, stir in 2 tbsp Pernod instead of the wine.

Garlic croûtes are traditionally served with fish soup; they can be made while the soup is simmering. Toast small slices of baguette, spread with garlic mayonnaise and sprinkle with grated cheese. Float in the hot soup just before serving.

Fast Fish Soup

1 leek, finely chopped

4 fat garlic cloves, crushed

3 celery sticks, finely chopped

1 small fennel bulb, finely chopped

1 red chilli, seeded and finely chopped (see page 14)

3 tbsp olive oil

50ml (2fl oz) dry white wine

about 750g (1lb 11oz) mixed fish and shellfish, such as haddock and monkfish fillets, peeled and deveined raw prawns, and fresh mussels, scrubbed and cleaned

4 tomatoes, chopped

20g (¾ oz) fresh thyme, chopped

salt and ground black pepper

1 Put the leek into a large pan, and add the garlic, celery, fennel, chilli and olive oil. Cook over a medium heat for 5 minutes or until the vegetables are soft and beginning to colour.

2 Stir in 1.1 litres (2 pints) boiling water and the wine. Bring to the boil, then cover and simmer for 5 minutes.

3 Cut the white fish into large chunks. Add to the soup with the tomatoes and thyme. Continue to simmer gently until the fish has just turned opaque. Add the prawns, simmer for 1 minute, then add the mussels, if you're using them.

4 As soon as all the mussels have opened (discard any that do not), season the soup with salt and pepper. Ladle into four warmed bowls and serve immediately.

Preparation Time: 10 minutes

Cooking Time: about 15 minutes

Serves: 4

Calories Per Serving: 269

1.4kg (3lb) full-flavoured tomatoes, preferably vine-ripened

2 red peppers, seeded and chopped

4 garlic cloves, crushed

3 small onions, thinly sliced

20g (³/₄oz) fresh thyme sprigs

4 tbsp olive oil

4 tbsp Worcestershire sauce

4 tbsp vodka

salt and ground black pepper

6 tbsp double cream to serve

Roasted Tomato and Pepper Soup

1 Preheat the oven to 200°C (180°C fan oven) mark 6. Put the tomatoes in a large roasting tin with the peppers, garlic and onions. Scatter 6 thyme sprigs over the top, drizzle with olive oil and roast in the oven for 25 minutes. Turn the vegetables over and roast for a further 30–40 minutes until tender and slightly charred.

2 Put one-third of the vegetables into a blender or food processor with 300ml (½ pint) freshly boiled water. Add the Worcestershire sauce and vodka, and season with salt and pepper. Whiz until smooth, then pass through a sieve into a pan.

3 Whiz the remaining vegetables with 450ml (³/₄ pint) freshly boiled water, then sieve and add to the pan.

4 To serve, warm the soup thoroughly, stirring occasionally. Pour into warmed bowls, add 1 tbsp double cream to each bowl, then drag a cocktail stick through the cream to swirl. Scatter a few fresh thyme leaves over the top and serve immediately.

Preparation Time: 20 minutes

Cooking Time: about 1 hour

Serves: 6

Calories Per Serving: 239

Cook's Tip

Serrano ham is Spanish cured ham, made in the same way as Parma ham.

1 x 225g jar marinated artichokes, drained and oil reserved

225g (8oz) firm goat's cheese, rind removed, diced

1 tbsp freshly chopped thyme leaves, plus extra thyme sprigs to garnish

grated zest of 1 lemon and 1 tbsp lemon juice

$\frac{1}{2}$ tsp wholegrain mustard

4 thick slices flavoured bread, such as olive or rosemary

75g (3oz) Serrano or Parma ham slices

salt and ground black pepper

olive oil to drizzle

crushed black pepper to garnish

Artichoke and Goat's Cheese Toasts

1 Halve the artichokes and put in a large bowl with the goat's cheese and chopped thyme.

2 Whisk together the lemon zest and juice, mustard and 3 tbsp of the reserved artichoke oil. Season with salt and pepper, whisk to combine, then stir into the artichoke mixture.

3 Toast the bread. Divide the artichoke mixture among the slices of toast and arrange the ham slices on top. Drizzle with a little olive oil, garnish with thyme sprigs and crushed black pepper and serve immediately.

Preparation Time: 15 minutes

Cooking Time: 3 minutes

Serves: 4

Calories Per Serving: 371

Freezing Tip

To freeze Complete the recipe, cool and put in a freezerproof container. Seal and freeze for up to three months.
To use Thaw for 4 hours at cool room temperature. Put in a pan, bring to the boil and simmer for 10 minutes.

1 tbsp olive oil

1 large onion, finely chopped

2 tsp coriander seeds, crushed

2 red chillies, seeded and chopped (see page 14)

1 butternut squash, about 750g (1lb 11oz), peeled and roughly chopped

2 sweet potatoes, peeled and roughly chopped

2 tomatoes, skinned and diced

1.7 litres (3 pints) hot vegetable stock

cheese straws to serve

Sweet Potato Soup

1 Heat the oil in a large pan over a gentle heat and fry the onion for about 10 minutes until soft. Add the coriander seeds and chillies to the pan and cook for 1–2 minutes.

2 Add the squash, sweet potatoes and tomatoes, and cook for 5 minutes. Add the hot stock, cover and bring to the boil. Simmer gently for 15 minutes or until the vegetables are soft. Using a blender, whiz the soup in batches until smooth. Reheat gently and serve with cheese straws.

Preparation Time: 20 minutes

Cooking Time: 35 minutes

Serves: 8

Calories Per Serving: 78

Mozzarella Mushrooms

8 large portobello mushrooms

8 slices marinated red pepper

8 fresh basil leaves

150g (5oz) mozzarella, cut into 8 slices

4 English muffins, halved

salt and ground black pepper

green salad to serve

1 Preheat the oven to 200°C (fan oven 180°C) mark 6. Lay the mushrooms side by side in a roasting tin and season with salt and pepper. Top each mushroom with a slice of red pepper and a basil leaf. Next, lay a slice of mozzarella on top of each mushroom. Season again. Roast in the oven for 15–20 minutes until the mushrooms are tender and the cheese has melted.

2 Meanwhile, toast the muffin halves until golden. Put a mozzarella mushroom on top of each muffin half. Serve immediately, with salad.

Preparation Time: 2–3 minutes

Cooking Time: 15–20 minutes

Serves: 4

Calories Per Serving: 137

Cook's Tip

Scrub mussels and clams before cooking to remove any grit or 'beards' from the shells.

2kg (4½ lb) fresh mussels, scrubbed, rinsed and beards removed

25g (1oz) butter

4 shallots, finely chopped

2 garlic cloves, crushed

200ml (7fl oz) dry white wine

2 tbsp freshly chopped flat-leafed parsley

100ml (3½ fl oz) single cream

salt and ground black pepper

crusty bread to serve

Moules Marinière

1 Tap the mussels on the worksurface, and discard any that do not close or have broken shells. Heat the butter in a large non-stick lidded pan, and sauté the shallots over a medium-high heat for about 10 minutes until soft.

2 Add the garlic, wine and half the parsley to the pan, and bring to the boil. Tip in the mussels and reduce the heat a little. Cover and cook for about 5 minutes or until all the shells have opened; discard any mussels that don't open.

3 Lift out the mussels with a slotted spoon and put into serving bowls; cover with foil to keep warm. Add the cream to the mussel liquid, season with salt and pepper, and cook for 1–2 minutes to heat through.

4 Pour a little sauce over the mussels and sprinkle with the rest of the parsley. Serve immediately with crusty bread.

Preparation Time: 15 minutes

Cooking Time: 20 minutes

Serves: 4

Calories Per Serving: 266

Cook's Tip

This is really two meals in one, a starter and a main course. The beef flavours the stock and is removed before serving. Later you divide up the meat and serve it with mashed potatoes, swedes or turnips.

1 piece of marrow bone, about 350g (12oz)

1.4kg (3lb) piece of beef skirt (ask your butcher for this)

300ml (½ pint) broth mix (pearl barley, red lentils, split peas and green peas), soaked according to the packet instructions

2 carrots, finely chopped

1 parsnip, finely chopped

2 onions, finely chopped

¼ white cabbage, finely chopped

1 leek, finely chopped

1–2 tbsp salt

ground black pepper

2 tbsp freshly chopped parsley to serve

Scotch Broth

1 Put the marrow bone and beef skirt into a 5.7 litre (10 pint) stock pot and add 2.6 litres (4½ pints) cold water – there should be enough to cover the meat.

2 Bring the water to the boil. Remove any scum from the surface with a spoon and discard. Reduce the heat to low, add the broth mix and simmer, partially covered, for 1½ hours, skimming the surface occasionally.

3 Add the carrots, parsnip, onions, cabbage, leek and another 600ml (1 pint) cold water. Cover to bring to the boil quickly, then simmer for 30 minutes.

4 Remove the marrow bone and piece of beef from the broth. Add a few shreds of beef to the broth if you like. Season the broth well with the salt and some pepper, stir in the chopped parsley and serve hot.

Preparation Time: 15 minutes

Cooking Time: 2 hours

Serves: 8

Calories Per Serving: 173

4 tbsp extra virgin olive oil

1 onion, finely chopped

2 garlic cloves, crushed

2 tsp freshly chopped thyme or
a large pinch of dried thyme

2 tsp freshly chopped rosemary
or a large pinch of dried rosemary

grated zest of ½ lemon

2 tsp ground coriander

¼ tsp cayenne pepper

125g (4oz) arborio (risotto) rice

1.1 litres (2 pints) vegetable stock

225g (8oz) fresh or frozen and thawed
spinach, shredded

4 tbsp pesto sauce

salt and ground black pepper

extra virgin olive oil and freshly grated Parmesan to serve

Spinach and Rice Soup

1 Heat half the oil in a pan. Add the onion, garlic, herbs, lemon zest and spices, then fry gently for 5 minutes.

2 Add the remaining oil with the rice and cook, stirring, for 1 minute. Add the stock, bring to the boil and simmer gently for 20 minutes or until the rice is tender.

3 Stir the spinach into the soup with the pesto sauce. Cook for 2 minutes, then season to taste with salt and pepper.

4 Serve drizzled with a little oil and topped with Parmesan.

Preparation Time: 10 minutes

Cooking Time: 25–30 minutes

Serves: 6

Calories Per Serving: 336

Thai Chicken Broth

1 tbsp olive oil

4 boneless skinless chicken thighs, around 300g (11oz), shredded

3 garlic cloves, roughly chopped

2 red chillies, seeded and finely diced (see page 14)

1 lemongrass stalk, finely sliced

5cm (2in) piece of fresh root ginger, finely chopped

150ml (¼ pint) white wine

1 litre (1¾ pints) chicken stock

8 fresh coriander sprigs

50g (2oz) rice noodles

125g (4oz) green beans, trimmed and halved

125g (4oz) bean sprouts

4 spring onions, finely sliced

2 tbsp Thai fish sauce (nam pla)

juice of ½ lime

salt and ground black pepper

1 Heat the oil in a large pan. Add the chicken, garlic, chillies, lemongrass and ginger, and cook over a medium heat for 3–5 minutes until the chicken is opaque.

2 Add the wine, bring to the boil and simmer until reduced by half. Add the stock and bring to the boil. Simmer for 5 minutes or until the chicken is cooked through.

3 Pick the leaves off the coriander and put them to one side. Finely chop the coriander stalks. Add the noodles to the pan and cook for 1 minute, then add the beans and coriander stalks. Cook for 3 minutes.

4 Add the bean sprouts and spring onions (reserving a few to garnish), fish sauce and lime juice. Bring to the boil and taste for seasoning. Ladle the broth into warmed bowls, making sure that each serving has some chicken and noodles. Garnish with the coriander leaves, spring onions and bean sprouts and serve.

Preparation Time: 20 minutes

Cooking Time: 20–25 minutes

Serves: 4

Calories Per Serving: 198

Freezing Tip

To freeze Complete the recipe to the end of step 2, then cool, pack and freeze for up to one month.
To use Thaw the soup overnight at cool room temperature, then complete the recipe.

Parsnip Soup with Chorizo

40g (1½oz) butter

1 onion, roughly chopped

225g (8oz) floury potatoes such as King Edward, peeled and chopped

400g (14oz) parsnips, peeled and chopped

4 tsp paprika, plus extra to dust

1.1 litres (2 pints) vegetable stock

450ml (¾ pint) milk

4 tbsp double cream

75g (3oz) sliced chorizo sausage, cut into fine strips

salt and ground black pepper

parsnip crisps and freshly grated Parmesan to serve

1 Melt the butter in a large heavy-based pan over a gentle heat. Add the onion and cook for 5 minutes until soft. Add the potatoes, parsnips and paprika. Mix well and cook gently, stirring occasionally, for 15 minutes or until the vegetables begin to soften.

2 Add the stock, milk and cream, and season with salt and pepper. Bring to the boil and simmer for about 25 minutes or until the vegetables are very soft. Add 50g (2oz) of the chorizo. Allow the soup to cool a little, then whiz in a blender or food processor until smooth. The soup can be thinned with additional stock or milk, if you like. Check the seasoning and put back in the pan.

3 To serve, reheat the soup. Serve in warmed bowls and top each with parsnip crisps; sprinkle with the remaining chorizo and a little Parmesan and dust with paprika.

Preparation Time: 20 minutes

Cooking Time: 1 hour

Serves: 8

Calories Per Serving: 278

130g pack cubed pancetta

50g (2oz) butter

3 leeks, about 450g (1lb), trimmed and thinly sliced

25g (1oz) plain flour

600ml (1 pint) milk

700g (1½lb) undyed smoked cod loin or haddock, skinned and cut into 2cm (¾in) cubes

326g can sweetcorn in water, drained

450g (1lb) small new potatoes, sliced

150ml (¼ pint) double cream

½ tsp paprika

salt and ground black pepper

2 tbsp freshly chopped flat-leafed parsley to garnish

Smoked Cod and Sweetcorn Chowder

1 Fry the pancetta in a large pan over a gentle heat until the fat runs out. Add the butter to the pan to melt, then add the leeks and cook until softened.

2 Stir in the flour and cook for a few seconds, then pour in the milk and 300ml (½ pint) cold water. Add the fish to the pan with the sweetcorn and potatoes. Bring to the boil and simmer for 10–15 minutes until the potatoes are cooked.

3 Stir in the cream, season with salt and pepper and the paprika, and cook for 2–3 minutes to warm through. Ladle into warmed shallow bowls and sprinkle each one with a little chopped parsley. Serve immediately.

Preparation Time: 5 minutes

Cooking Time: 20 minutes

Serves: 6

Calories Per Serving: 517

2 tbsp vegetable oil

500g (1lb 2oz) shelled large scallops,
cut into 5mm (1/4 in) slices

4 celery sticks, sliced diagonally

1 bunch of spring onions, sliced diagonally

25g (1oz) piece fresh root ginger, peeled and sliced

2 large garlic cloves, sliced

1/4 tsp chilli powder

2 tbsp lemon juice

2 tbsp light soy sauce

3 tbsp freshly chopped coriander

salt and ground black pepper

Scallops with Ginger

1 Heat the oil in a wok or large frying pan.
Add the scallops, celery, spring onions, ginger,
garlic and chilli powder and stir-fry over a high
heat for 2 minutes or until the vegetables are
just tender.

2 Pour in the lemon juice and soy sauce, allow
to bubble up, then stir in about 2 tbsp chopped
coriander and season with salt and pepper.
Serve immediately, sprinkled with the remaining
coriander.

Preparation Time: 15 minutes

Cooking Time: 3 minutes

Serves: 6

Calories Per Serving: 197

375g pack ready-rolled puff pastry
(preferably made with butter)

1 medium egg, beaten

2 tbsp coarse sea salt

300g (11oz) vegetable antipasti in oil (mixed roasted peppers,
artichokes, onions, etc)

a little olive oil (if needed)

2 tbsp balsamic vinegar

200g (7oz) red pepper hummus

50g (2oz) wild rocket

salt and ground black pepper

Roasted Vegetable and Rocket Tartlets

1 Preheat the oven to 220°C (200°C fan oven) mark 7. Unroll the puff pastry on a lightly floured surface and cut it into six equal-sized squares.

2 Lay the pastry squares on a large baking sheet and prick each one all over with a fork. Brush all over with the beaten egg, and sprinkle the edges of each square with sea salt. Bake in the oven for 5–7 minutes until the pastry is golden brown and cooked through.

3 Pour off 4 tbsp olive oil from the antipasti (you may need to add a little extra olive oil) into a bowl. Add the balsamic vinegar. Season well with salt and pepper, then put to one side.

4 To serve, divide the hummus among the six pastry bases, spreading it over each one. Put each pastry square on an individual plate and spoon over the vegetable antipasti – there's no need to be neat. Whisk the balsamic vinegar dressing together, add the rocket leaves and toss to coat, then pile a small handful of leaves on top of each tartlet. Serve immediately.

Preparation Time: 15 minutes

Cooking Time: 5–7 minutes

Serves: 6

Calories Per Serving: 387

Simple Suppers

Spicy Bean and Tomato Fajitas

Lamb Chops with Crispy Garlic Potatoes

Baked Fish

Mushroom, Bacon and Leek Risotto

One-pan Chicken with Tomatoes

Sweet Chilli Beef Stir-fry

Salmon with Roasted Vegetables

Mixed Mushroom Frittata

Spicy Beans with Jazzed-up Potatoes

Quick and Easy Carbonara

Oven-poached Cod with Herbs

Quick Steak Supper

Chicken Stir-fry with Noodles

Tuna Melt Pizza

Pasta with Pesto and Beans

Stuffed Chicken Breasts

Black-eye Bean Chilli

Salmon Kedgeree

Chicken with Oyster Sauce

Lemon Chicken

Potato and Chorizo Tortilla

Chicken Curry with Rice

Roast Tomato Pasta

Flash-in-the-pan Pork

Beef with Mushrooms and Oyster Sauce

Spicy Sausage and Pasta Supper

Stir-fried Pork with Chinese Greens

Pesto Gnocchi

Fish and Chips

Steak and Chips

Quick Chicken Stir-fry

Teriyaki Salmon with Spinach

Stir-fried Pork with Egg Noodles

Simple Smoked Haddock

Spicy Bean and Tomato Fajitas

2 tbsp sunflower oil

1 onion, sliced

2 garlic cloves, crushed

½ tsp hot chilli powder

1 tsp ground coriander

1 tsp ground cumin

1 tbsp tomato purée

400g can chopped tomatoes

225g can red kidney beans, drained and rinsed

300g can borlotti beans, drained and rinsed

300g can flageolet beans, drained and rinsed

150ml (¼ pint) hot vegetable stock

2 ripe avocados, quartered and chopped

juice of ½ lime

1 tbsp freshly chopped coriander, plus extra sprigs to garnish

6 ready-made flour tortillas

150ml (5 fl oz) soured cream

salt and ground black pepper

lime wedges to serve

1 Heat the oil in a large pan. Add the onion and cook gently for 5 minutes. Add the garlic and spices and cook for a further 2 minutes.

2 Add the tomato purée and cook for 1 minute, then add the tomatoes, beans and hot stock. Season well with salt and pepper, bring to the boil and simmer for 15 minutes, stirring occasionally.

3 Put the avocado into a bowl, add the lime juice and the chopped coriander, and mash together. Season to taste.

4 To warm the tortillas, either wrap them in foil and heat in the oven at 180°C (160°C fan oven) mark 4 for 10 minutes, or put on a plate and microwave on full power for 45 seconds.

5 Spoon the beans down the centre of each tortilla. Add a little avocado and soured cream, then fold the two sides in so that they overlap. Garnish with coriander sprigs and serve with lime wedges.

Preparation Time: 15 minutes

Cooking Time: 25 minutes

Serves: 6

Calories Per Serving: 508

Cook's Tip

Make your own mint sauce: finely chop 20g ($^3/_4$oz) fresh mint and mix with 1 tbsp each olive oil and white wine vinegar.

Lamb Chops with Crispy Garlic Potatoes

2 tbsp mint sauce

8 small lamb chops

3 medium potatoes, peeled and cut into 5mm ($^1/_4$ in) slices

2 tbsp garlic-flavoured olive oil

1 tbsp olive oil

salt and ground black pepper

steamed green beans to serve

1 Spread the mint sauce over the lamb chops and leave to marinate while you prepare the potatoes.

2 Boil the potatoes in a pan of lightly salted water for 2 minutes until just starting to soften. Drain, tip back into the pan, season with salt and pepper and toss through the garlic oil.

3 Meanwhile, heat the olive oil in a large frying pan and fry the chops for 4–5 minutes on each side until just cooked, adding a splash of boiling water to the pan to make a sauce. Remove the chops and sauce from the pan and keep warm.

4 Add the potatoes to the pan. Fry over a medium heat for 10–12 minutes until crisp and golden. Divide the potatoes, chops and sauce among four plates and serve with green beans.

Preparation Time: 10 minutes

Cooking Time: 20 minutes

Serves: 4

Calories: 835

1 small butternut squash, peeled and cut into small cubes

½ red onion, finely sliced

2 garlic cloves, finely chopped

1 tbsp roughly chopped dill, plus extra sprigs to garnish

1 tbsp olive oil

4 thick haddock or salmon fillets, about 150g (5oz) each

125g (4oz) fresh spinach

salt and ground black pepper

lemon wedges to serve

Baked Fish

1 Preheat the oven to 220°C (200°C fan) mark 7. Cut out four 40.5cm (16in) squares of foil.

2 Put the squash in a bowl. Add the onion, garlic, dill and oil, and toss to coat. Season well with salt and pepper. Divide the vegetable mixture among the four squares of foil.

3 Top each pile of vegetables with a piece of fish. Season again, then bring the foil together and crimp the edges so that the fish and vegetables are completely enclosed. Put the parcels on a baking tray and roast for 15 minutes or until the fish is cooked through and the squash is just tender.

4 Carefully open each of the foil parcels and add the spinach. Close again and roast for a further 5 minutes or until the spinach has wilted. Garnish with dill and serve with lemon wedges to squeeze over the fish.

Preparation Time: 10 minutes

Cooking Time: 20 minutes

Serves: 4

Calories Per Serving: 191

Cook's Tip

To enrich the flavour, add a splash of dry sherry or white wine to the pan when you add the rice.

Mushroom, Bacon and Leek Risotto

25g (1oz) dried mushrooms

250g (9oz) dry-cure smoked bacon, rind removed, chopped

3 leeks, chopped

300g (11oz) risotto rice

20g (³/₄oz) chives, chopped

25g (1oz) freshly grated Parmesan, plus extra to sprinkle

1 Put the mushrooms in a large heatproof bowl and pour over 1.4 litres (2½ pints) boiling water. Leave to soak for 10 minutes.

2 Meanwhile, fry the bacon and leeks in a large pan – no need to add oil – for 7–8 minutes until soft and golden.

3 Stir in the rice, cook for 1–2 minutes, then add the mushrooms and their soaking liquid. Cook at a gentle simmer, stirring occasionally, for 15–20 minutes until the rice is cooked and most of the liquid has been absorbed.

4 Stir in the chives and grated Parmesan. Divide among four warmed bowls, then sprinkle with extra Parmesan to serve.

Preparation Time: 10 minutes

Cooking Time: about 30 minutes

Serves: 4

Calories Per Serving: 452

Try Something Different

Use flageolet beans or other canned beans instead of mixed beans and garnish with fresh basil or oregano.

One-pan Chicken with Tomatoes

4 chicken thighs

1 red onion, sliced

400g can chopped tomatoes with herbs

400g can mixed beans

2 tsp balsamic vinegar

freshly chopped flat-leafed parsley to garnish

1 Heat a non-stick pan and fry the chicken thighs, skin side down, until golden. Turn over and fry for 5 minutes.

2 Add the onion and fry for 5 minutes. Add the tomatoes, beans and balsamic vinegar. Cover and simmer for 10–12 minutes until piping hot. Garnish with parsley and serve immediately.

Preparation Time: 5 minutes

Cooking Time: 20–25 minutes

Serves: 4

Calories Per Serving: 238

Try Something Different

Other vegetables are just as good: try pak choi, baby sweetcorn, courgettes or carrots cut into thin strips.

1 tsp chilli oil

1 tbsp soy sauce

1 tbsp clear honey

1 garlic clove, crushed

1 large red chilli, halved, seeded and chopped (see page 14)

400g (14oz) lean beef, cut into strips

1 tsp sunflower oil

1 broccoli head, sliced into small florets

200g (7oz) mangetouts, halved

1 red pepper, halved, seeded and cut into strips

Sweet Chilli Beef Stir-fry

1 Put the chilli oil in a medium-sized shallow bowl. Add the soy sauce, honey, garlic and chilli, and stir well. Add the strips of beef and toss in the marinade.

2 Heat the sunflower oil in a wok over a high heat until it is very hot. Cook the strips of beef in two batches, then remove them from the pan and keep warm. Wipe the pan with kitchen paper to remove any residue.

3 Add the broccoli, mangetouts, red pepper and 2 tbsp water. Stir-fry for 5–6 minutes until starting to soften. Return the beef to the pan to heat through. Serve immediately.

Preparation Time: 10 minutes

Cooking Time: 15 minutes

Serves: 4

Calories Per Serving: 273

Salmon with Roasted Vegetables

2 large leeks, cut into chunks

2 large courgettes, sliced

2 fennel bulbs, cut into chunks

125ml (4fl oz) hot vegetable stock

grated zest of ½ lemon

4 salmon fillets, 100g (3½ oz) each

15g (½ oz) pinenuts, toasted

salt and ground black pepper

1 Preheat the oven to 200°C (180°C fan oven) mark 6. Put the leeks into a roasting tin. Add the courgettes and fennel. Pour over the stock, season well with salt and pepper and roast for 30 minutes or until tender.

2 Meanwhile, sprinkle the lemon zest over the salmon and season. Put on a baking sheet lined with greaseproof paper and cook in the oven with the vegetables for the last 20 minutes of the cooking time.

3 Scatter the pinenuts over the roasted vegetables and mix together well. Divide the vegetables among four plates and top each with a piece of salmon. Serve immediately.

Preparation Time: 10 minutes

Cooking Time: 30 minutes

Serves: 6

Calories Per Serving: 258

Mixed Mushroom Frittata

1 tbsp olive oil

300g (11oz) mixed mushrooms, sliced

2 tbsp freshly chopped thyme

grated zest and juice of ½ lemon

50g (2oz) watercress, chopped

6 medium eggs, beaten

salt and ground black pepper

1 Heat the oil in a large deep frying pan over a medium heat. Add the mushrooms and thyme, and stir-fry for 4–5 minutes until starting to soften and brown. Stir in the lemon zest and juice, then bubble for 1 minute. Lower the heat.

2 Preheat the grill. Add the watercress to the beaten eggs, season with salt and pepper and pour into the pan. Cook on the hob for 7–8 minutes until the sides and base are firm but the centre is still a little soft.

3 Transfer to the grill and cook for 4–5 minutes until just set. Cut into wedges and serve hot.

Preparation Time: 15 minutes

Cooking Time: 15–20 minutes

Serves: 4

Calories Per Serving: 14

Try Something Different

The spicy beans are just as good served with toast for a quick meal that takes less than 25 minutes.

Spicy Beans with Jazzed-up Potatoes

4 baking potatoes

1 tbsp olive oil, plus extra to rub

1 tsp smoked paprika, plus a pinch

2 shallots, finely chopped

1 tbsp freshly chopped rosemary

400g can cannellini beans, drained and rinsed

400g can chopped tomatoes

1 tbsp light muscovado sugar

1 tsp Worcestershire sauce

75ml (2½fl oz) red wine

75ml (2½fl oz) hot vegetable stock

2 tbsp freshly chopped flat-leafed parsley

grated mature Cheddar cheese to sprinkle

sea salt and ground black peppe

1 Preheat the oven to 200°C (180°C fan oven) mark 6. Rub the potatoes with a little oil and put them on a baking tray. Scatter some sea salt over and a pinch of smoked paprika. Bake for 1–1½ hours until tender.

2 Meanwhile, heat 1 tbsp oil in a large pan, add the shallots and fry over a low heat for 1–2 minutes until they start to soften.

3 Add the rosemary and 1 tsp paprika, and fry for 1–2 minutes, then add the beans, tomatoes, sugar, Worcestershire sauce, red wine and stock. Season, then bring to the boil and simmer, uncovered, for 10–15 minutes. Serve with the baked potatoes, scattered with parsley and grated Cheddar cheese.

Preparation Time: 12 minutes

Cooking Time: about 1½ hours

Serves: 4

Calories Per Serving: 298

350g (12oz) tagliatelle

150g (5oz) smoked bacon, chopped

1 tbsp olive oil

2 large egg yolks

150ml (¼ pint) double cream

50g (2oz) freshly grated Parmesan

2 tbsp freshly chopped parsley

Quick and Easy Carbonara

1 Bring a large pan of water to the boil. Add the pasta, bring back to the boil and cook for 4 minutes or according to the packet instructions.

2 Meanwhile, fry the bacon in the oil for 4–5 minutes. Add to the drained pasta and keep hot.

3 Put the egg yolks in a bowl and add the cream. Whisk together. Add to the pasta with the Parmesan and parsley. Toss well and serve immediately.

Preparation Time: 5 minutes

Cooking Time: 10 minutes

Serves: 4

Calories Per Serving: 688

Try Something Different

There are lots of alternatives to cod: try sea bass, gurnard or pollack.

Oven-poached Cod with Herbs

10 spring onions, sliced

2 garlic cloves, crushed

6 tbsp shredded fresh mint

6 tbsp freshly chopped flat-leafed parsley

juice of ½ lemon

150ml (¼ pint) fish, chicken or vegetable stock

4 cod fillets, about 200g (7oz) each

salt and ground black pepper

1 Preheat the oven to 230°C (210°C fan oven) mark 8. Combine the spring onions, garlic, mint, parsley, lemon juice and stock in an ovenproof dish that can hold the cod in a single layer.

2 Put the cod on the herb and garlic mixture, and turn to moisten. Season with salt and pepper, and roast for 8–10 minutes until the fish is cooked. Serve immediately.

Preparation Time: 10 minutes

Cooking Time: 10 minutes

Serves: 4

Calories Per Serving: 170

Try Something Different

Instead of ciabatta, serve the steak with tagliatelle or other pasta.

Quick Steak Supper

2 sirloin steaks

3 tsp olive oil

4 large mushrooms, sliced

1 red onion, sliced

1 tbsp Dijon mustard

25g (1oz) butter

2 ciabattas, halved lengthways,
then quartered, to make eight pieces

salt and ground black pepper

green salad to serve

1 Heat a griddle or large frying pan until very hot. Rub the steaks with 1 tsp olive oil, season with salt and pepper, and fry for about 2 minutes on each side if you like your steak rare, or 4 minutes each side for medium. Remove from the pan and leave to 'rest'.

2 Heat the remaining oil in the pan. Add the mushrooms and onion. Fry, stirring, for 5 minutes until softened. Stir in the mustard and butter, and take off the heat.

3 Toast the ciabatta on both sides. Thinly slice the steaks and divide among four pieces of ciabatta. Top with the mushrooms, onion and remaining ciabatta and serve with salad.

Preparation Time: 10 minutes

Cooking Time: about 10 minutes

Serves: 4

Calories Per Serving: 452

Try Something Different

Use turkey or pork escalopes instead of the chicken: you will need 450g (1lb), cut into thin strips.

Chicken Stir-fry with Noodles

2 tbsp vegetable oil

2 garlic cloves, crushed

4 skinless, boneless chicken breasts, each sliced into 10 pieces

3 medium carrots, about 450g (1lb), cut into thin strips, about 5cm (2in) long

250g pack thick egg noodles

1 bunch spring onions, sliced

200g (7oz) mangetouts, ends trimmed

155g jar sweet chilli and lemongrass sauce

1 Fill a large pan with water and bring to the boil. Meanwhile, heat the oil in a wok or frying pan, then add the garlic and stir-fry for 1–2 minutes. Add the chicken pieces and stir-fry for 5 minutes, then add the carrot strips and stir-fry for a further 5 minutes.

2 Put the noodles into the boiling water and cook according to the packet instructions.

3 Meanwhile, add the spring onions, mangetouts and sauce to the wok. Stir-fry for 5 minutes.

4 Drain the cooked noodles well and add to the wok. Toss everything together and serve.

Preparation Time: 20 minutes

Cooking Time: 20 minutes

Serves: 4

Calories Per Serving: 355

Try Something Different

Mozzarella and Tomato Spread the pizza bases with 4 tbsp pesto and top with 125g (4oz) chopped sunblush tomatoes and 2 x 125g sliced mozzarella balls. Cook, then serve topped with a handful of baby spinach leaves.

Ham and Pineapple Spread the pizza bases with 4 tbsp tomato pasta sauce. Top with a 225g can drained unsweetened pineapple chunks, 125g (4oz) diced ham and 125g (4oz) grated Gruyère.

Tuna Melt Pizza

1 Preheat the oven to 220°C (200°C fan oven) mark 7. Spread each pizza base with 2 tbsp sun-dried tomato pesto. Top each with half the tuna, half the anchovies and half the grated cheese.

2 Put on to a baking sheet and cook in the oven for 10–12 minutes until the cheese has melted. Sprinkle with rocket to serve.

2 large pizza bases

4 tbsp sun-dried tomato pesto

2 x 185g cans tuna, drained

50g can anchovies, drained and chopped

125g (4oz) grated mature Cheddar cheese

rocket to serve

Preparation Time: 5 minutes

Cooking Time: 10–12 minutes

Serves: 4

Calories Per Serving: 688

Cook's Tip

This combination of pasta, potatoes, green beans and pesto is a speciality of Liguria on the East coast of Italy. Traditionally, it is made with the twisted pasta shape known as trofie (see photograph) – pieces of pasta are rolled on a flat surface until they form rounded lengths of pasta with tapered ends. Each length is then twisted into its final shape.

Pasta with Pesto and Beans

350g (12oz) trofie or other dried pasta shapes

175g (6oz) fine green beans, roughly chopped

175g (6oz) small salad potatoes, such as Anya, thickly sliced

250g (9oz) fresh pesto sauce

freshly grated Parmesan to serve

1 Bring a large pan of water to the boil. Add the pasta, bring back to the boil and cook for 5 minutes.

2 Add the beans and potatoes to the pan and continue to boil for a further 7–8 minutes until the potatoes are just tender.

3 Drain the pasta, beans and potatoes in a colander, then tip everything back into the pan and stir in the pesto sauce. Serve scattered with freshly grated Parmesan.

Preparation Time: 5 minutes

Cooking Time: 15 minutes

Serves: 4

Calories Per Serving: 738

Cook's Tip

Sage has a naturally strong, pungent taste, so you only need a little to flavour the chicken. Don't be tempted to add more than just one leaf to each chicken breast as too much will overpower the finished dish.

Stuffed Chicken Breasts

oil to grease

150g (5oz) ball mozzarella

4 chicken breasts, about 150g (5oz) each

4 sage leaves

8 slices Parma ham

1 Preheat the oven to 200°C (180°C fan oven) mark 6. Lightly grease a baking sheet. Slice the mozzarella into eight, then put two slices on each chicken breast. Top each with a sage leaf. Season with freshly ground black pepper.

2 Wrap each piece of chicken in two slices of Parma ham, covering the mozzarella.

3 Put on to the baking sheet and cook in the oven for 20 minutes or until the chicken is cooked through.

Preparation Time: 5 minutes

Cooking Time: 20 minutes

Serves: 4

Calories Per Serving: 297

Try Something Different

Replace half the black-eye beans with red kidney beans.

Black-eye Bean Chilli

1 tbsp olive oil

1 onion, chopped

3 celery sticks, finely chopped

2 x 400g cans black-eye beans, drained

2 x 400g cans chopped tomatoes

2 or 3 splashes of Tabasco sauce

3 tbsp freshly chopped coriander

warm tortillas and soured cream to serve

1 Heat the olive oil in a heavy-based frying pan over a low heat. Add the onion and celery, and fry for 10 minutes until softened.

2 Add the black-eye beans to the pan with the tomatoes and Tabasco sauce. Bring to the boil, then simmer for 10 minutes.

3 Just before serving, stir in the chopped coriander. Spoon the chilli on to warm tortillas, and serve with a spoonful of soured cream.

Preparation Time: 10 minutes

Cooking Time: 20 minutes

Serves: 4

Calories Per Serving: 245

Try Something Different

Instead of salmon, use undyed smoked haddock fillet.

50g (2oz) butter

700g (1½lb) onions, sliced

2 tsp garam masala

1 garlic clove, crushed

75g (3oz) split green lentils, soaked in 300ml (½ pint) boiling water for 15 minutes, then drained

750ml (1¼ pints) hot vegetable stock

225g (8oz) basmati rice

1 green chilli, seeded and finely chopped (see page 14)

350g (12oz) salmon fillet

salt and ground black pepper

Salmon Kedgeree

1 Melt the butter in a flameproof casserole over a medium heat. Add the onions and cook for 5 minutes or until soft. Remove a third of the onions and put to one side. Increase the heat and cook the remaining onions for 10 minutes to caramelise. Remove and put to one side.

2 Put the first batch of onions back in the casserole, add the garam masala and garlic, and cook, stirring, for 1 minute. Add the drained lentils and stock, cover and cook for 15 minutes. Add the rice and chilli, and season with salt and pepper. Bring to the boil, cover and simmer for 5 minutes.

3 Put the salmon fillet on top of the rice, cover and continue to cook gently for 15 minutes or until the rice is cooked, the stock absorbed and the salmon opaque.

4 Lift off the salmon and divide into flakes. Put it back in the casserole, and fork through the rice. Garnish with the reserved caramelised onion and serve.

Preparation Time: 15 minutes, plus 15 minutes soaking

Cooking Time: 55 minutes

Serves: 4

Calories Per Serving: 490

Try Something Different

Instead of chicken, try this with thinly sliced pork tenderloin.

Chicken with Oyster Sauce

6 tbsp vegetable oil

450g (1lb) skinless chicken breast fillets, cut into bite-size pieces

3 tbsp oyster sauce

1 tbsp dark soy sauce

100ml (3½fl oz) chicken stock

2 tsp lemon juice

1 garlic clove, thinly sliced

6–8 large flat mushrooms, about 250g (9oz) total weight, sliced

125g (4oz) mangetouts

1 tsp cornflour mixed with 1 tbsp water

1 tbsp sesame oil

salt and ground black pepper

1 Heat 3 tbsp oil in a wok or large frying pan. Add the chicken and cook over a high heat, stirring continuously for 2–3 minutes until lightly browned. Remove the chicken with a slotted spoon and drain on kitchen paper.

2 In a bowl, mix the oyster sauce with the soy sauce, chicken stock and lemon juice. Add the chicken and mix thoroughly.

3 Heat the remaining vegetable oil in the pan over a high heat and stir-fry the garlic for about 30 seconds; add the mushrooms and cook for 1 minute. Add the chicken mixture, cover and simmer for 8 minutes.

4 Stir in the mangetouts and cook for a further 2–3 minutes. Remove the pan from the heat and stir in the cornflour mixture. Return the pan to the heat, add the sesame oil and stir until the sauce has thickened. Season with salt and pepper and serve immediately.

Preparation Time: 10 minutes

Cooking Time: 15–20 minutes

Serves: 4

Calories Per Serving: 330

Try Something Different

Instead of lemons, use limes. Knead them on the worktop for 30 seconds before squeezing so they give as much juice as possible.

Lemon Chicken

4 small chicken breasts, cut into chunky strips

juice of 2 lemons

2 tbsp olive oil

4–6 tbsp demerara sugar

salt

green salad to serve

1 Put the chicken in a large bowl and season with salt. Add the lemon juice and olive oil and stir to mix.

2 Preheat the grill to medium. Spread the chicken on a large baking sheet, and sprinkle over half the sugar. Grill for 3–4 minutes until caramelised, then turn the chicken over, sprinkle with the remaining sugar and grill until the chicken is cooked through and golden.

3 Divide the chicken among four plates, and serve with a green salad.

Preparation Time: 2 minutes

Cooking Time: 6–8 minutes

Serves: 4

Calories Per Serving: 231

Potato and Chorizo Tortilla

6 tbsp olive oil

450g (1lb) potatoes, very thinly sliced

225g (8oz) onions, thinly sliced

2 garlic cloves, finely chopped

50g (2oz) sliced chorizo, cut into thin strips

6 large eggs, lightly beaten

salt and ground black pepper

1 Heat the oil in an 18cm (7in) non-stick frying pan over a medium-low heat. Add the potatoes, onions and garlic. Stir together until coated in the oil, then cover the pan. Cook gently, stirring from time to time, for 10–15 minutes until the potato is soft. Season with salt, then add the chorizo.

2 Preheat the grill until hot. Season the beaten eggs with salt and pepper, and pour over the potato mixture. Cook over a medium heat for 5 minutes or until beginning to brown at the edges and the egg is about three-quarters set. Put the pan under the grill to brown the top. The egg should be a little soft in the middle, as it continues to cook and set as it cools.

3 Carefully loosen the tortilla around the edge and underneath with a flexible turner or spatula. Cut into wedges and serve warm or at room temperature.

Preparation Time: 5 minutes

Cooking Time: 25 minutes

Serves: 4

Calories Per Serving: 431

2 tbsp vegetable oil

1 onion, finely sliced

2 garlic cloves, crushed

6 skinless chicken thigh fillets, cut into strips

2 tbsp tikka masala curry paste

200g can chopped tomatoes

450ml (¾ pint) hot vegetable stock

200g (7oz) basmati rice

1 tsp salt

225g (8oz) baby leaf spinach

poppadums and mango chutney to serve

Chicken Curry with Rice

1 Heat the oil in a large pan, add the onion and fry over a medium heat for about 5 minutes until golden. Add the garlic and chicken, and stir-fry for about 5 minutes until golden.

2 Add the curry paste, tomatoes and stock. Stir and bring to the boil, then cover with a lid and simmer over a low heat for 15 minutes or until the chicken is cooked (cut a piece in half to check that it's white all the way through).

3 Meanwhile, cook the rice. Put 600ml (1 pint) water in a medium pan, cover and bring to the boil. Add the rice and salt, and stir. Replace the lid and turn down the heat to its lowest setting. Cook for the time stated on the pack. Once cooked, cover with a teatowel and the lid. Leave for 5 minutes to absorb the steam.

4 Add the spinach to the curry and cook until just wilted.

5 Spoon the rice into bowls, add the curry and serve with poppadums and mango chutney.

Preparation Time: 20 minutes

Cooking Time: 25 minutes, plus 5 minutes standing

Serves: 4

Calories Per Serving: 453

400g (14oz) dried rigatoni pasta

700g (1½lb) cherry tomatoes

olive oil to drizzle

50g (2oz) pinenuts

a large handful of fresh basil leaves, torn

salt and ground black pepper

freshly grated Parmesan to serve

Roast Tomato Pasta

1 Preheat the oven to 240°C (220°C fan oven) mark 9. Bring a large pan of lightly salted water to the boil. Add the pasta, cover and bring back to the boil. Remove the lid and cook the pasta according to the packet instructions.

2 Meanwhile, cut half the tomatoes in two and arrange them in a large roasting tin, cut side up. Add the remaining whole tomatoes and drizzle all with olive oil. Season with salt and pepper. Put the pinenuts on to a separate roasting tray, and roast both in the oven for 15 minutes until the tomatoes are softened and lightly caramelised. Watch carefully to make sure the pinenuts don't scorch, and remove from the oven earlier if necessary.

3 Drain the pasta well and add to the roasting tin when the tomatoes are done. Scatter over the basil and pinenuts, then stir thoroughly to coat the pasta in the juices. Adjust the seasoning, and stir in a little more olive oil if you like. Sprinkle with Parmesan and serve.

Preparation Time: 5 minutes

Cooking Time: 15 minutes

Serves: 4

Calories Per Serving: 507

Flash-in-the-pan Pork

700g (1½ lb) new potatoes, scrubbed, halved if large

175g (6oz) runner beans, sliced

a little sunflower or olive oil

4 pork escalopes

150ml (¼ pint) hot chicken stock

150ml (¼ pint) cider

2 tbsp wholegrain mustard

150g (5oz) Greek yogurt

4 fresh tarragon stems, leaves only

a squeeze of lemon juice

1 Cook the potatoes in a pan of boiling salted water for 10 minutes. Add the beans and cook for a further 5 minutes or until tender. Drain.

2 Meanwhile, heat the oil in a large non-stick frying pan over a medium heat, and cook the pork for 3 minutes on each side until browned. Remove from the pan and keep warm. Add the stock, cider and mustard to the pan, increase the heat and bubble to reduce the liquid by half.

3 Just before serving, reduce the heat and add the yogurt, tarragon leaves and lemon juice. Put the pork back in the pan to coat with the sauce and warm through. Serve with the potatoes and beans.

Preparation Time: 5 minutes

Cooking Time: 15 minutes

Serves: 4

Calories Per Serving: 346

175–225g (6–8oz) rump steak, cut into thin strips

2 tbsp oyster sauce

2 tbsp dry sherry

25g (1oz) dried black or shiitake mushrooms soaked in boiling water for 30 minutes

2 tbsp vegetable oil

1 small onion, thinly sliced

1 garlic clove, crushed

2.5cm (1in) piece fresh root ginger, peeled and cut into thin strips

2 carrots, cut into matchsticks

2 tsp cornflour

salt and ground black pepper

rice to serve

Preparation Time: 15 minutes, plus soaking and marinating

Cooking Time: about 15 minutes

Serves: 4

Calories Per Serving: 390

Beef with Mushrooms and Oyster Sauce

1 Put the steak, oyster sauce and sherry in a bowl and add salt and pepper to taste. Stir well to mix, then cover and marinate in the refrigerator for 30 minutes. Drain the mushrooms and reserve the soaking liquid. Squeeze the mushrooms dry; discard any hard stalks.

2 Heat the oil in a wok or large frying pan. Add the onion and garlic and stir-fry gently for about 5 minutes until soft but not coloured.

3 Add the mushrooms, ginger and carrots to the pan and stir-fry over medium heat for about 6 minutes until slightly softened. Remove the vegetables with a slotted spoon and set aside.

4 Add the beef and marinade to the pan and stir-fry for 2–3 minutes, until the beef is tender. Mix the cornflour with 4 tbsp of the soaking water from the mushrooms. Pour the mixture into the pan, put the vegetables back in and stir-fry until the sauce is thickened. Taste and adjust the seasoning with salt and pepper, if necessary. Serve immediately, with boiled rice.

Get Ahead

To prepare ahead Complete the recipe to the end of step 2, cool quickly, cover and chill for up to one day.
To use Bring back to the boil, stir in the pasta and complete the recipe.

1 tbsp olive oil

200g (7oz) salami, sliced

225g (8oz) onion, finely chopped

50g (2oz) celery, finely chopped

2 garlic cloves, crushed

400g can pimientos, drained, rinsed and chopped

400g (14oz) passata or 400g can chopped tomatoes

125g (4oz) sun-dried tomatoes in oil, drained

600ml (1 pint) hot chicken or vegetable stock

300ml (½ pint) red wine

1 tbsp sugar

75g (3oz) dried pasta shapes

400g can borlotti beans, drained and rinsed

salt and ground black pepper

300ml (½ pint) soured cream to serve

175g (6oz) Parmesan, freshly grated, to serve (optional)

freshly chopped flat-leafed parsley to garnish

Spicy Sausage and Pasta Supper

1 Heat the oil in a large pan over a medium heat and fry the salami for 5 minutes or until golden and crisp. Drain on kitchen paper.

2 Fry the onion and celery in the hot oil for 10 minutes or until soft and golden. Add the garlic and fry for 1 minute. Put the salami back in the pan with the pimientos, passata or chopped tomatoes, sun-dried tomatoes, stock, red wine and sugar. Bring to the boil.

3 Stir in the pasta, bring back to the boil and cook for about 10 minutes or according to the packet instructions until the pasta is almost tender.

4 Stir in the beans and simmer for 3–4 minutes. Top up with more stock if the pasta is not tender when the liquid has been absorbed. Season with salt and pepper.

5 Ladle into warmed bowls and serve topped with soured cream and garnished with the chopped parsley. Serve the grated Parmesan separately.

Preparation Time: 15 minutes

Cooking Time: 30 minutes

Serves: 6

Calories Per Serving: 629

Get Ahead

To prepare ahead Complete to the end of step 3, then cool, wrap and chill the pork and vegetables separately for up to four hours.
To use Complete the recipe until the pork is piping hot.

Stir-fried Pork with Chinese Greens

200g (7oz) pork tenderloin or fillet, cut into strips

2 tbsp finely chopped fresh root ginger

3 tbsp soy sauce

2 garlic cloves, crushed

700g (1½lb) mixed vegetables, such as pak choi, broccoli, carrots, bean sprouts and sugarsnap peas

3 tbsp vegetable oil

5 spring onions, cut into four lengthways

1 red chilli, seeded and sliced (see page 14)

1 tbsp sesame oil

2 tbsp dry sherry

2 tbsp oyster sauce

salt and ground black pepper

1 Put the pork in a non-metallic dish with the ginger, 2 tbsp soy sauce and the garlic. Set aside to marinate for at least 30 minutes.

2 Meanwhile, prepare the vegetables. Cut the pak choi into quarters, separate the broccoli into florets and cut the carrot into ribbons, using a vegetable peeler.

3 Heat a wok or large frying pan over a high heat and add the vegetable oil. Stir-fry the pork, in two batches, for 2–3 minutes until the meat is browned. Season the pork with salt and pepper, set aside and keep warm.

4 Add the spring onions and chilli to the pan and cook for 30 seconds. Add all the vegetables and stir-fry for 4–5 minutes. Return the pork to the pan. Add the remaining soy sauce, sesame oil, sherry and oyster sauce, then stir-fry for 2 minutes or until the sauce is syrupy. Serve immediately.

Preparation Time: 15 minutes, plus 30 minutes marinating

Cooking Time: about 15 minutes

Serves: 4

Calories: 234

Pesto Gnocchi

800g (1lb 12oz) fresh gnocchi

200g (7oz) green beans, trimmed and chopped

125g (4oz) fresh green pesto

10 sunblush tomatoes, roughly chopped

1 Cook the gnocchi in a large pan of lightly salted boiling water according to the packet instructions. Add the beans to the water for the last 3 minutes of cooking time.

2 Drain the gnocchi and beans and put back in the pan. Add the pesto and tomatoes and toss well. Serve immediately.

Preparation Time: 10 minutes

Cooking Time: about 10 minutes

Serves: 4

Calories Per Serving: 481

Try Something Different

Simple Tartare Sauce Mix 8 tbsp mayonnaise with 1 tbsp each chopped capers and gherkins, 1 tbsp freshly chopped tarragon or chives and 2 tsp lemon juice.
Herby Lemon Mayonnaise Fold 2 tbsp finely chopped parsley, grated zest of ½ lemon and 2 tsp lemon juice into 8 tbsp mayonnaise.

Fish and Chips

900g (2lb) Desiree, Maris Piper or King Edward potatoes, peeled

2–3 tbsp olive oil

sea salt flakes

sunflower oil to deep-fry

2 x 128g packs batter mix

1 tsp baking powder

¼ tsp salt

330ml bottle of lager

4 plaice fillets, about 225g (8oz) each, skin on, trimmed and cut in half

plain flour to dust

2 garlic cloves, crushed

8 tbsp mayonnaise

1 tsp lemon juice

salt and ground black pepper

lemon wedges and chives to garnish

1 Preheat the oven to 220°C (200°C fan oven) mark 7. Put the potato chips into a pan of lightly salted water. Bring to the boil, then simmer for 4–5 minutes. Drain well.

2 Put the chips into a roasting tin, toss with 1 tbsp olive oil and cook in the oven, turning once, for 30–40 minutes until golden and cooked through.

3 Meanwhile, half-fill a deep-fat fryer with sunflower oil and heat to 190°C. Put the batter mix into a bowl with the baking powder and salt, and gradually whisk in the lager. Season the plaice and lightly dust with flour. Dip two of the fillets into the batter and deep-fry in the hot oil until golden. Keep hot in the oven while you deep-fry the remaining fish.

4 Mix the garlic, mayonnaise and lemon juice together in a bowl and season well. Serve the garlic mayonnaise with the plaice and chips, garnished with lemon wedges and chives.

Preparation Time: 30 minutes

Cooking Time: 40–50 minutes

Serves: 4

Calories Per Serving: 993

2 large potatoes, peeled and cut into chips

2 tbsp olive oil

4 sirloin steaks, 125g (4oz) each, fat trimmed

25g (1oz) Roquefort cheese, cut into four small pieces

salt and ground black pepper

watercress to garnish

Steak and Chips

1 Preheat the oven to 220°C (200°C fan oven) mark 7. Put the potato chips into a pan of lightly salted water. Bring to the boil, then simmer for 4–5 minutes. Drain well.

2 Put the chips into a roasting tin, toss with 1 tbsp olive oil and cook in the oven, turning once, for 30–40 minutes until golden and cooked through.

3 When the chips are nearly done, heat a non-stick frying pan until really hot. Brush the remaining oil over the steaks and season with salt and pepper. Add to the pan and fry for 2–3 minutes on each side for medium rare, or 2 minutes more if you prefer the meat well done. Put on to warmed plates, top each steak with a small piece of Roquefort while still hot and serve with the chips. Garnish with watercress.

Preparation Time: 10 minutes

Cooking Time: 35–45 minutes

Serves: 4

Calories Per Serving: 318

Try Something Different

Other vegetables are just as good in this dish: try pak choi, button mushrooms, carrots cut into matchsticks, or baby sweetcorn.

Quick Chicken Stir-fry

1 tsp groundnut oil

300g (11oz) skinless chicken breast fillets, sliced

4 spring onions, chopped

200g (7oz) medium rice noodles

100g (3½oz) mangetouts

200g (7oz) purple sprouting broccoli, chopped

2–3 tbsp sweet chilli sauce

freshly chopped coriander and lime wedges (optional) to garnish

1 Heat the oil in a wok or large frying pan and add the chicken and spring onions. Stir-fry over a high heat for 5–6 minutes until the chicken is golden.

2 Meanwhile, soak the rice noodles in boiling water for 4 minutes or according to the packet instructions.

3 Add the mangetouts, broccoli and chilli sauce to the chicken. Continue to stir-fry for 4 minutes.

4 Drain the noodles and add them to the pan. Toss everything together. Scatter the chopped coriander over the top and serve with lime wedges to squeeze over, if you like.

Preparation Time: 10 minutes

Cooking Time: 12 minutes

Serves: 4

Calories Per Serving: 316

Cook's Tip

Furikake seasoning is a Japanese condiment consisting of sesame seeds and chopped seaweed; it can be found in major supermarkets and Asian food shops.

Soba noodles are made from buckwheat and are gluten-free. If you have a wheat allergy or gluten intolerance, look for 100% soba on the pack.

Teriyaki Salmon with Spinach

550g (1¼ lb) salmon fillet, cut into 1cm (½ in) slices

3 tbsp teriyaki sauce

3 tbsp tamari or light soy sauce

2 tbsp vegetable oil

1 tbsp sesame oil

1 tbsp chopped fresh chives

2 tsp grated fresh root ginger

2 garlic cloves, crushed

350g (12oz) soba noodles (see Cook's Tip)

350g (12oz) baby spinach leaves

furikake seasoning (see Cook's Tip)

1 Gently mix the salmon slices with the teriyaki sauce, then cover, chill and leave to marinate for 1 hour.

2 Mix together the soy sauce, 1 tbsp vegetable oil, sesame oil, chives, ginger and garlic. Set aside.

3 Cook the noodles according to the packet instructions. Drain and put to one side.

4 Heat the remaining vegetable oil in a wok or large frying pan. Remove the salmon from the marinade and add it to the pan. Cook over a high heat until it turns opaque – about 30 seconds. Remove from the pan and put to one side.

5 Add the drained noodles to the pan and stir until warmed through. Stir in the spinach and cook for 1–2 minutes until wilted. Add the soy sauce mixture and stir to combine.

6 Divide the noodles among four deep bowls, then top with the salmon. Sprinkle with furikake seasoning and serve.

Preparation Time: 10 minutes, plus 1 hour marinating

Cooking Time: 6 minutes

Serves: 4

Calories Per Serving: 672

Cook's Tip

Creamed Coconut is a solid white block of coconut which can be added directly in chunks to sauces or reconstituted with water.

Stir-fried Pork with Egg Noodles

150g (5oz) medium egg noodles

450g (1lb) pork escalope, cut into thin strips

2 tsp soy sauce

4–6 tbsp sunflower oil

125g (4oz) carrots, cut into matchsticks

225g (8oz) broccoli, cut into florets

150g (5oz) sugarsnap peas, halved diagonally

125g (4oz) mushrooms, thickly sliced

1 bunch of spring onions, thinly sliced

3 tbsp Thai green curry paste

150g (5oz) creamed coconut, roughly chopped and melted in 300ml (½ pint) boiling water (see Cook's Tip)

150ml (¼ pint) chicken stock

Thai fish sauce (optional)

salt and ground black pepper

1 Bring a pan of water to the boil and cook the noodles for 4 minutes or according to the packet instructions. Drain, then plunge into cold water. Set aside.

2 Season the pork with salt, pepper and soy sauce. Heat 1 tbsp oil in a wok or large frying pan. Fry the pork in two batches over a high heat, cooking each batch for 2–3 minutes until lightly browned, adding extra oil if necessary. Remove and set aside.

3 Heat 3 tbsp oil and stir-fry the carrots, broccoli and sugarsnap peas for 2–3 minutes. Add the mushrooms and spring onions, reserving a few to garnish, and fry for 1–2 minutes. Remove and set aside.

4 Add the curry paste, coconut and chicken stock to the pan. Bring to the boil and simmer for 5 minutes. Drain the noodles and add to the pan with the pork and vegetables. Stir well, bring to the boil and simmer for 1–2 minutes to heat through. Season with salt and pepper and a splash of fish sauce, if you like. Serve immediately, garnished with spring onions.

Preparation Time: 15 minutes

Cooking Time: 20 minutes

Serves: 4

Calories Per Serving: 778

Cook's Tip

Smoked fish is quite salty so always taste the sauce before seasoning with any extra salt.

25g (1oz) unsalted butter

1 tbsp olive oil

1 garlic clove, thinly sliced

4 thick smoked haddock or cod fillets, about 175g (6oz) each

a small handful of freshly chopped parsley (optional)

finely grated zest of 1 small lemon, plus lemon wedges to serve

romanesco, cauliflower or broccoli to serve

Simple Smoked Haddock

1 Heat the butter, oil and garlic in a large non-stick pan over a high heat until the mixture starts to foam and sizzle. Put the fish into the pan, skin side down, and fry for 10 minutes – this will give a golden crust underneath the fish.

2 Carefully turn the fish over. Scatter the parsley, if using, and lemon zest over each fillet, then fry for a further 30 seconds. Put a cooked fillet on each of four warmed plates, and spoon over some of the buttery juices. Serve with the lemon wedges and steamed romanesco, cauliflower or broccoli.

Preparation Time: 10 minutes

Cooking Time: about 10 minutes

Serves: 4

Calories Per Serving: 217

Hearty Meals

Cook's Tip

Leeks can trap a lot of fine soil, so need to be washed thoroughly: trim the ends of the leaves, then cut a cross about 7.5cm (3in) into the top and rinse well under cold running water.

Braised Beef

175g (6oz) smoked pancetta or smoked streaky bacon, cut into cubes

2 medium leeks, thickly sliced

1 tbsp olive oil

450g (1lb) braising steak, cut into 5cm (2in) pieces

1 large onion, finely chopped

2 carrots and 2 parsnips, thickly sliced

1 tbsp plain flour

300ml (10fl oz) red wine

300ml (10fl oz) water

1–2 tbsp redcurrant jelly

ground black pepper

125g (4oz) chestnut mushrooms, halved

freshly chopped flat-leafed parsley to garnish

1 Preheat the oven to 170°C (150°C fan oven) mark 3. Fry the pancetta or bacon in a shallow flameproof casserole for 2–3 minutes until golden. Add the leeks and cook for a further 2 minutes or until the leeks are just beginning to colour. Remove with a slotted spoon and put to one side.

2 Heat the oil in the casserole and fry the beef in batches for 2–3 minutes until a rich golden colour on all sides. Remove from the casserole and set aside. Add the onion and fry over a gentle heat for 5 minutes or until golden. Stir in the carrots and parsnips and fry for 1–2 minutes.

3 Put the beef back into the casserole and stir in the flour to soak up the juices. Gradually add the red wine and water, then stir in the redcurrant jelly. Season with pepper and bring to the boil. Cover with a tight-fitting lid and cook in the oven for 2 hours.

4 Stir in the fried leeks, pancetta and mushrooms, re-cover and cook for a further 1 hour or until everything is tender. Serve scattered with chopped parsley.

Preparation Time: 20 minutes,

Cooking Time: about 3½ hours

Serves: 4

Calories Per Serving: 490

Cook's Tip

Tamarind paste has a very sharp, sour flavour and is widely used in Asian and South-east Asian cooking.

2 tbsp vegetable oil

2 onions, finely sliced

2 garlic cloves, crushed

1 tbsp ground coriander

1 tsp mild chilli powder

1 tbsp black mustard seeds

2 tbsp tamarind paste

2 tbsp sun-dried tomato paste

750g (1lb 11oz) new potatoes, quartered

400g can chopped tomatoes

1 litre (1¾ pints) hot vegetable stock

250g (9oz) green beans, trimmed

2 x 400g cans chickpeas, drained and rinsed

2 tsp garam masala

salt and ground black pepper

Chickpea Curry

1 Heat the oil in a pan and fry the onions for 10–15 minutes until golden – when they have a good colour they will add depth of flavour. Add the garlic, coriander, chilli, mustard seeds, tamarind paste and sun-dried tomato paste. Cook for 1–2 minutes until the aroma from the spices is released.

2 Add the potatoes and toss in the spices for 1–2 minutes. Add the tomatoes and stock, and season with salt and pepper. Cover and bring to the boil. Simmer, half covered, for 20 minutes or until the potatoes are just cooked.

3 Add the beans and chickpeas, and continue to cook for 5 minutes or until the beans are tender and the chickpeas are warmed through. Stir in the garam masala and serve.

Preparation Time: 20 minutes

Cooking Time: 40–45 minutes

Serves: 6

Calories Per Serving: 291

Try Something Different

Replace the lamb chops with 4 chicken legs; cook for 30–35 minutes until cooked through. Uncover and cook for a further 15 minutes.

Spiced Lamb with Lentils

1 tbsp sunflower oil

8 lamb chops, trimmed of fat

2 onions, finely sliced

1 tsp paprika

1 tsp ground cinnamon

400g can lentils, drained

400g can chickpeas, drained

300ml (½ pint) lamb or chicken stock

salt and ground black pepper

freshly chopped flat-leafed parsley to garnish

1 Preheat the oven to 180°C (160°C fan oven) mark 4. Heat the oil in a large non-stick frying pan, add the chops and brown on both sides. Remove from the pan with a slotted spoon.

2 Add the onions, paprika and cinnamon to the pan. Fry for 2–3 minutes. Stir in the lentils and chickpeas. Season with salt and pepper, then spoon into a shallow 2 litre (3½ pint) ovenproof dish.

3 Put the chops on top of the onion and lentil mixture and pour the stock over them.

4 Cover the dish tightly and cook in the oven for 1½ hours or until the chops are tender. Uncover and cook for 30 minutes or until lightly browned. Scatter over the parsley and serve hot.

Preparation Time: 10 minutes

Cooking Time: 2¼ hours

Serves: 4

Calories Per Serving: 315

1.8kg (4lb) free-range chicken

25g (1oz) butter, softened

2 tbsp olive oil

1 lemon, cut in half

1 small head of garlic, cut in half horizontally

salt and ground black pepper

Perfect Roast Chicken

1 Preheat the oven to 220°C (200°C fan oven) mark 7. Put the chicken in a roasting tin just large enough to hold it comfortably. Spread the butter all over the chicken, then drizzle with the oil and season with salt and pepper.

2 Squeeze the lemon juice over it, then put one lemon half inside the chicken. Put the other half and the garlic into the roasting tin.

3 Put the chicken into the oven for 15 minutes then turn the heat down to 190°C (170°C fan oven) mark 5 and cook for a further 45 minutes–1 hour until the leg juices run clear when pierced with a skewer or sharp knife. While the bird is cooking, baste from time to time with the pan juices. Add a splash of water to the tin if the juices dry out.

4 Take the chicken out, put on a warm plate and cover with foil. Leave for 10 minutes before carving, so the juices that have risen to the surface soak back into the meat. This will make it more moist and easier to slice. Mash some of the garlic into the pan juices and serve the gravy with the chicken.

Preparation Time: 5 minutes

Cooking Time: 1 hour–1¼ hours, plus resting

Serves: 4

Calories Per Serving: 639

Try Something Different

There are lots of alternatives to cod and haddock: try sea bass, gurnard, coley (saithe) or pollack.

Fish Stew

2 tbsp olive oil

1 onion, chopped

1 leek, chopped

2 tsp smoked paprika

2 tbsp tomato purée

450g (1lb) cod or haddock, roughly chopped

125g (4oz) basmati rice

175ml (6fl oz) white wine

450ml (¾ pint) hot fish stock

200g (7oz) cooked peeled king prawns

a large handful of spinach leaves

crusty bread to serve

1 Heat the oil in a large pan. Add the onion and leek and fry for 8–10 minutes until they start to soften. Add the smoked paprika and tomato purée, and cook for 1–2 minutes.

2 Add the fish, rice, wine and stock. Bring to the boil, then cover and simmer for 10 minutes or until the fish is cooked through and the rice is tender. Add the prawns, cook for 1 minute until heated through, stir in the spinach and serve with chunks of bread.

Preparation Time: 15 minutes

Cooking Time: about 30 minutes

Serves: 4

Calories Per Serving: 280

50g (2oz) fresh breadcrumbs

450g (1lb) minced lean pork

1 tsp fennel seeds, crushed

¼ tsp chilli flakes, or to taste

3 garlic cloves, crushed

4 tbsp freshly chopped flat-leafed parsley

3 tbsp red wine

roughly chopped fresh oregano to garnish

spaghetti to serve

For the tomato sauce

oil-water spray (see page 105)

2 large shallots, finely chopped

3 pitted black olives, shredded

2 garlic cloves, crushed

2 pinches of chilli flakes

250ml (9fl oz) vegetable or chicken stock

500g carton passata

2 tbsp each freshly chopped flat-leafed parsley, basil and oregano

salt and ground black pepper

Italian Meatballs

1 To make the tomato sauce, spray a pan with the oil-water spray and add the shallots. Cook gently for 5 minutes. Add the olives, garlic, chilli flakes and stock. Bring to the boil, cover and simmer for 3–4 minutes.

2 Uncover and simmer for 10 minutes or until the shallots and garlic are soft and the liquid syrupy. Stir in the passata and season with salt and pepper. Bring to the boil and simmer for 10–15 minutes, then stir in the herbs.

3 Meanwhile, put the breadcrumbs, pork and remaining ingredients into a large bowl, season and mix together, using your hands, until thoroughly combined. (If you wish to check the seasoning, fry a little mixture, taste and adjust if necessary.)

4 Preheat the grill. With wet hands, roll the meat mixture into balls. Line a grill pan with foil, shiny side up, and spray with oil-water spray. Cook the meatballs under the preheated grill for 3–4 minutes on each side. Serve with the tomato sauce and spaghetti, garnished with oregano.

Preparation Time: 15 minutes

Cooking Time: 50 minutes

Serves: 4

Calories Per Serving: 275

Cook's Tip

Fresh lasagne sheets wrapped around a filling are used here to make a cannelloni, but you can also buy dried cannelloni tubes, which can easily be filled using a teaspoon.

Mixed Mushroom Cannelloni

Preparation Time: 15 minutes

Cooking Time: 50–55 minutes

Serves: 4

Calories Per Serving: 631

6 sheets fresh lasagne

3 tbsp olive oil

1 small onion, finely sliced

3 garlic cloves, sliced

20g pack fresh thyme, finely chopped

225g (8oz) chestnut or brown-cap mushrooms, roughly chopped

125g (4oz) flat-cap mushrooms, roughly chopped

2 x 125g goat's cheese logs, with rind

350g carton cheese sauce

salt and ground black pepper

1   Preheat the oven to 180°C (160°C fan oven) mark 4. Cook the lasagne in boiling water until just tender. Drain well and run under cold water. Keep covered with cold water until ready to use.

2   Heat the oil in a large pan and add the onion. Cook over a medium heat for 7–10 minutes until the onion is soft. Add the garlic and fry for 1–2 minutes. Keep a few slices of garlic to one side. Keep a little thyme for sprinkling over later, then add the rest to the pan with the mushrooms. Cook for a further 5 minutes or until the mushrooms are golden brown and there is no excess liquid in the pan. Season, remove from the heat and set aside.

3   Crumble one of the goat's cheese logs into the cooled mushroom mixture and stir together. Drain the lasagne sheets and pat dry with kitchen paper. Spoon 2–3 tbsp of the mushroom mixture along the long edge of each lasagne sheet, leaving a 1cm (½in) border. Roll up the pasta sheets and cut each roll in half. Put the pasta in a shallow ovenproof dish and spoon over the cheese sauce. Slice the remaining goat's cheese into rounds and arrange over the pasta rolls. Sprinkle the reserved garlic and thyme on top. Cook for 30–35 minutes until golden and bubbling.

Cook's Tip

Queen green olives are large, meaty olives with a mild flavour.

Spanish Chicken Parcels

12 boneless, skinless chicken thighs, about 900g (2lb)

180g jar pimientos or roasted red peppers, drained

12 thin slices chorizo sausage

2 tbsp olive oil

1 onion, finely chopped

4 garlic cloves, crushed

225g can chopped tomatoes

4 tbsp dry sherry

18 Queen green olives

salt and ground black pepper

1 Put the chicken thighs on a board, season well with salt and pepper and put a piece of pimiento inside each one. Wrap a slice of chorizo around the outside and secure with two cocktail sticks. Put to one side.

2 Heat the olive oil in a pan over a medium heat, and fry the onion for 10 minutes. Add the garlic and cook for 1 minute. Put the chicken parcels, chorizo-side down, in the pan and brown them all over for 10–15 minutes.

3 Add the chopped tomatoes and sherry to the pan and bring to the boil. Simmer for 5 minutes or until the chicken juices run clear when pierced with a skewer. Add the olives and warm through. Remove the cocktail sticks and serve.

Preparation Time: 15 minutes

Cooking Time: about 30 minutes

Serves: 6

Calories Per Serving: 444

Cook's Tip

To make a quick salsa, peel and roughly chop ½ ripe avocado. Put in a bowl with 4 roughly chopped tomatoes, 1 tsp olive oil and the juice of ½ lime. Mix well.

One-pot Spicy Beef

2 tsp sunflower oil

1 large onion, roughly chopped

1 garlic clove, finely chopped

1 small red chilli, finely chopped (see page 14)

2 red peppers, roughly chopped

2 celery sticks, diced

400g (14oz) lean beef mince

400g can chopped tomatoes

2 x 400g cans mixed beans, drained

1–2 tsp Tabasco sauce

2–3 tbsp roughly chopped fresh coriander to garnish (optional)

salsa (see Cook's Tip) and soft flour tortillas or basmati rice to serve

1 Heat the oil in a large heavy-based frying pan over a medium heat. Add the onion to the pan with 2 tbsp water. Cook for 10 minutes or until soft. Add the garlic and chilli, and cook for a further 1–2 minutes until golden. Add the red peppers and celery, and cook for 5 minutes.

2 Add the beef to the pan and brown all over. Add the tomatoes, beans and Tabasco sauce, then simmer for 20 minutes. Garnish with coriander, if you like, and serve with salsa and tortillas or rice.

Preparation Time: 10 minutes

Cooking Time: 40 minutes

Serves: 4

Calories Per Serving: 478

50g (2oz) butter

400g (14oz) leeks, trimmed and sliced

1 onion, chopped

1 tbsp olive oil

800g (1lb 12oz) casserole lamb, cubed and tossed with 1 tbsp plain flour

2 garlic cloves, crushed

800g (1lb 12oz) waxy potatoes such as Desirée, peeled and sliced

3 tbsp freshly chopped parsley

1 tsp freshly chopped thyme

600ml (1 pint) lamb stock

150ml (¼ pint) double cream

salt and ground black pepper

Lamb and Leek Hotpot

1 Melt half the butter in a 3.5 litre (6¼ pint) flameproof casserole dish over a low heat. Add the leeks and onion, stir to coat, then cover and cook for 10 minutes. Remove and put to one side.

2 Add the oil to the casserole and heat, then brown the meat in batches with the garlic and plenty of salt and pepper. Remove and put to one side.

3 Preheat the oven to 170°C (150°C fan oven) mark 3. Put half the potatoes in a layer over the bottom of the casserole and season with salt and pepper. Add the reserved meat, then the leek mixture. Arrange a layer of overlapping potatoes on top of that, sprinkle with the parsley and thyme, then pour in the stock.

4 Bring the casserole to the boil, cover, then cook on a low shelf in the oven for about 1 hour 50 minutes. Remove the lid, dot with the rest of the butter and add the cream. Cook uncovered for 30–40 minutes until the potatoes are golden brown.

Preparation Time: 20 minutes

Cooking Time: 2 hours 50 minutes

Serves: 6

Calories Per Serving: 549

2 tsp vegetable oil

1 green chilli, seeded and finely chopped (see page 14)

4cm (1½ in) piece fresh root ginger, peeled and finely grated

1 lemongrass stalk, cut into 3 pieces

225g (8oz) brown-cap or oyster mushrooms

1 tbsp Thai green curry paste

300ml (½ pint) coconut milk

150ml (¼ pint) chicken stock

1 tbsp Thai fish sauce

1 tsp light soy sauce

350g (12oz) skinless chicken breast fillets, cut into bite-size pieces

350g (12oz) cooked peeled large prawns

fresh coriander sprigs to garnish

Thai Green Curry

1 Heat the oil in a wok or large frying pan, add the chilli, ginger, lemongrass and mushrooms and stir-fry for about 3 minutes or until the mushrooms begin to turn golden. Add the curry paste and fry for a further 1 minute.

2 Pour in the coconut milk, stock, fish sauce and soy sauce and bring to the boil. Stir in the chicken and simmer for about 8 minutes or until the chicken is cooked. Add the prawns and cook for a further 1 minute. Garnish with coriander sprigs and serve immediately.

Preparation Time: 10 minutes

Cooking Time: 15 minutes

Serves: 6

Calories Per Serving: 132

Turkish Lamb Stew

2 tbsp olive oil

400g (14oz) lean lamb fillet, cubed

1 red onion, sliced

1 garlic clove, crushed

1 potato, quartered

400g can chopped tomatoes

1 red pepper, seeded and sliced

200g (7oz) canned chickpeas, drained and rinsed

1 aubergine, cut into chunks

200ml (7fl oz) lamb stock

1 tbsp red wine vinegar

1 tsp each freshly chopped thyme, rosemary and oregano

salt and ground black pepper

1 Heat 1 tbsp olive oil in a flameproof casserole and brown the lamb over a high heat. Reduce the heat and add the remaining oil, the onion and garlic, then cook until soft.

2 Preheat the oven to 170°C (150°C fan oven) mark 3. Add the potato, tomatoes, red pepper, chickpeas, aubergine, stock, vinegar and herbs to the pan. Season with salt and pepper, stir and bring to the boil. Cover the pan, transfer to the oven and cook for 1–1½ hours until the lamb is tender.

Preparation Time: 10 minutes

Cooking Time: 1½–2 hours

Serves: 4

Calories Per Serving: 389

Try Something Different

Add a drained 225g can of bamboo shoots with the other vegetables in step 2, if you like.

Hot Jungle Curry

1 tbsp vegetable oil

350g (12oz) skinless chicken breast fillets, cut into 5cm (2in) strips

2 tbsp Thai red curry paste

2.5cm (1in) piece fresh root ginger, peeled and thinly sliced

125g (4oz) aubergine, cut into bite-size pieces

125g (4oz) baby sweetcorn, halved lengthways

75g (3oz) green beans, trimmed

75g (3oz) button or brown-cap mushrooms, halved if large

2–3 kaffir lime leaves (optional)

450ml (¾ pint) chicken stock

2 tbsp Thai fish sauce

grated zest of ½ lime, plus extra to garnish

1 tsp tomato purée

1 tbsp soft brown sugar

1 Heat the oil in a wok or large frying pan. Add the chicken and cook, stirring, for 5 minutes or until the chicken turns golden brown.

2 Add the curry paste and cook for a further 1 minute. Add the ginger, aubergine, sweetcorn, beans, mushrooms and lime leaves, if using, and stir until coated in the curry paste. Add all the remaining ingredients and bring to the boil. Simmer gently for 10–12 minutes or until the chicken and vegetables are just tender. Serve immediately, sprinkled with lime zest.

Preparation Time: 10 minutes

Cooking Time: 18–20 minutes

Serves: 4

Calories Per Serving: 160

3 tbsp olive oil

400g (14oz) pork escalopes, cubed

1 red onion, sliced

2 leeks, cut into chunks

2 celery sticks, cut into chunks

1 tbsp harissa paste

1 tbsp tomato purée

400g (14oz) cherry tomatoes

300ml (¼ pint) hot vegetable or chicken stock

400g can cannellini beans, drained and rinsed

1 marinated red pepper, sliced

salt and ground black pepper

freshly chopped flat-leafed parsley to garnish

Greek yogurt, lemon wedges and bread to serve

Spicy Pork and Bean Stew

1 Preheat the oven to 180°C (160°C fan oven) mark 4. Heat 2 tbsp oil in a flameproof casserole and fry the pork in batches until golden. Remove from the pan and set aside.

2 Heat the remaining oil in the pan and fry the onion for 5–10 minutes until softened. Add the leeks and celery, and cook for about 5 minutes. Return the pork to the pan, and add the harissa and tomato purée. Cook for 1–2 minutes, stirring all the time. Add the tomatoes and stock and season well with salt and pepper. Bring to the boil, then transfer to the oven and cook for 25 minutes.

3 Add the drained beans and red pepper to the mixture and put back in the oven for 5 minutes to warm through. Garnish with parsley and serve with a dollop of Greek yogurt, lemon wedges for squeezing over, and chunks of crusty baguette or wholegrain bread.

| **Preparation Time:** 15 minutes |
| **Cooking Time:** 50–55 minutes |
| **Serves:** 4 |
| **Calories Per Serving:** 348 |

Try Something Different

Use mixed beans instead of the butter beans.

1 tbsp olive oil

12 chicken pieces (6 drumsticks and 6 thighs)

175g (6oz) Spanish chorizo sausage, cubed

1 onion, finely chopped

2 large garlic cloves, crushed

1 tsp mild chilli powder

3 red peppers, cut in half, seeded and roughly chopped

400g (14oz) passata

2 tbsp tomato purée

300ml (½ pint) chicken stock

2 x 400g cans butter beans, drained and rinsed

200g (7oz) baby new potatoes, halved

1 small bunch thyme

1 bay leaf

200g (7oz) baby leaf spinach

Chicken with Chorizo and Beans

1 Preheat the oven to 190°C (170°C fan oven) mark 5. Heat the oil in a large flameproof casserole and brown the chicken all over. Remove from the pan and set aside. Add the chorizo to the casserole and fry for 2–3 minutes until its oil starts to run.

2 Add the onion, garlic and chilli powder, and fry over a low heat for 5 minutes or until soft.

3 Add the peppers and cook for 2–3 minutes until soft. Stir in the passata, tomato purée, stock, beans, potatoes, thyme sprigs and bay leaf. Cover and simmer for 10 minutes.

4 Return the chicken and any juices to the casserole. Bring to a simmer, then cover and cook in the oven for 30–35 minutes. If the sauce looks thin, return the casserole to the hob over a medium heat and simmer to reduce until nicely thick.

5 Remove the thyme and bay leaf, and stir in the spinach until it wilts. Serve immediately.

Preparation Time: 10 minutes

Cooking Time: about 1 hour 10 minutes

Serves: 6

Calories Per Serving: 690

Cook's Tip

If you can't find Desiree potatoes, use Maris Piper or King Edward instead.

Sausages with Roasted Onions and Potatoes

900g (2lb) Desiree potatoes, cut into wedges

4 tbsp olive oil

3–4 fresh rosemary sprigs (optional)

2 red onions, each cut into 8 wedges

8 sausages

salt and ground black pepper

1 Preheat the oven to 220°C (200°C fan oven) mark 7. Put the potatoes in the roasting tin – they should sit in one layer. Drizzle over the oil and season with salt and pepper. Toss well to coat the potatoes in oil, then put the rosemary on top, if using, and roast in the oven for 20 minutes.

2 Remove the roasting tin from the oven and add the onion wedges. Toss again to coat the onions and turn the potatoes. Put the sausages among the potatoes and onions. Return the tin to the oven for 1 hour.

3 Divide among four plates and serve immediately.

Preparation Time: 10 minutes

Cooking Time: 1 hour 20 minutes

Serves: 4

Calories Per Serving: 640

Lamb and Pasta Pot

1 half leg of lamb roasting joint – about 1.1kg (2½lb) total weight

125g (4oz) smoked streaky bacon, chopped

150ml (¼ pint) red wine

400g can chopped tomatoes with chilli, or passata

75g (3oz) dried pasta shapes

12 sunblush tomatoes

150g (5oz) char-grilled artichokes in oil, drained and halved

a handful of basil leaves to garnish

1 Preheat the oven to 200°C (180°C fan oven) mark 6. Put the lamb and bacon in a small, deep roasting tin and fry over a medium-high heat for 5 minutes or until the lamb is brown all over and the bacon is beginning to crisp.

2 Remove the lamb and set aside. Pour the wine into the tin with the bacon – it should bubble immediately. Stir well, scraping the base to loosen any crusty bits, then leave to bubble until half the wine has evaporated. Stir in 300ml (½ pint) water and add the chopped tomatoes or passata, pasta and sunblush tomatoes.

3 Put the lamb on a rack over the roasting tin so that the juices drip into the pasta. Cook, uncovered, in the oven for about 35 minutes.

4 Stir the artichokes into the pasta and put everything back in the oven for 5 minutes or until the lamb is tender and the pasta cooked. Slice the lamb thickly. Serve with the pasta and scatter the basil on top.

Preparation Time: 10 minutes

Cooking Time: 50 minutes

Serves: 4

Calories Per Serving: 686

Try Something Different

Omit the baby new potatoes and serve with mashed potatoes.

1 small chicken

1 fresh rosemary sprig

2 bay leaves

1 red onion, cut into wedges

2 carrots, cut into chunks

2 leeks, cut into chunks

2 celery sticks, cut into chunks

12 baby new potatoes

900ml (1½ pints) hot vegetable stock

200g (7oz) green beans, trimmed

Easy Chicken Casserole

1 Preheat the oven to 180°C (160°C fan oven) mark 4. Put the chicken and herbs in a large flameproof casserole. Add the onion, carrots, leeks, celery, potatoes and stock. Bring to the boil, then cook in the oven for 45 minutes or until the chicken is cooked. To test, pierce the thickest part of the leg with a skewer or knife; the juices should run clear.

2 Add the beans and cook for 5 minutes. Spoon the vegetables into six bowls. Carve the chicken and divide among the bowls, and ladle the stock over.

Preparation Time: 15 minutes

Cooking Time: 50 minutes

Serves: 6

Calories Per Serving: 323

Freezing Tip

Freeze at step 3 for up to one month.
To use Cook from frozen on a Swiss roll tin at 200°C (180°C fan oven) mark 6 for 45 minutes.

Cook's Tip

Traditional Parmesan is not strictly vegetarian, as it contains calves' rennet. However, most supermarkets now stock a vegetarian version.

Classic Nut Roast

40g (1½oz) butter

1 onion, finely chopped

1 garlic clove, crushed

125g (4oz) fresh white breadcrumbs

grated zest and juice of ½ lemon

225g (8oz) mixed white nuts, such as Brazil nuts, macadamia nuts, pinenuts and almonds, ground in a food processor

75g (3oz) vegetarian sage Derby or Parmesan cheese, grated

125g (4oz) canned peeled chestnuts, roughly chopped

½ x 400g can artichoke hearts, roughly chopped

1 medium egg, lightly beaten

2 tsp each freshly chopped parsley, sage and thyme, plus extra fresh sprigs

salt and ground black pepper

steamed mixed vegetables to serve

1 Preheat the oven to 200°C (180°C fan oven) mark 6. Melt the butter in a pan and cook the onion and garlic for 5 minutes or until soft. Put into a large bowl and set aside to cool.

2 Add the breadcrumbs, lemon zest and juice, ground nuts, grated cheese, chestnuts and artichokes. Season well with salt and pepper and bind the mixture together with the beaten egg. Stir in the freshly chopped herbs.

3 Put the mixture on to a large buttered piece of foil and shape into a fat, tightly packed rough sausage. Scatter over the extra herb sprigs and wrap in the foil.

4 Cook on a Swiss roll tin for 30–40 minutes, then unwrap the foil slightly and cook for a further 15 minutes until it turns golden. Cut into thick slices and serve with steamed vegetables.

Preparation Time: 20 minutes, plus cooling

Cooking Time: about 1 hour

Serves: 8

Calories Per Serving: 386

Beef Stroganoff

700g (1½lb) rump or fillet steak, trimmed

50g (2oz) unsalted butter or 4 tbsp olive oil

1 onion, thinly sliced

225g (8oz) brown-cap mushrooms, sliced

3 tbsp brandy

1 tsp French mustard

200ml (7fl oz) crème fraîche

100ml (3½fl oz) double cream

3 tbsp freshly chopped flat-leafed parsley

salt and ground black pepper

rice or noodles to serve

1 Cut the steak into strips about 5mm (¼in) wide and 5cm (2in) long.

2 Heat half the butter or olive oil in a large heavy frying pan over a medium heat. Add the onion and cook gently for 10 minutes or until soft and golden; remove with a slotted spoon and put to one side. Add the mushrooms to the pan and cook, stirring, for 2–3 minutes until golden brown; remove and put to one side.

3 Increase the heat and quickly fry the meat, in two or three batches, for 2–3 minutes, stirring constantly to ensure even browning. Add the brandy and let bubble to reduce.

4 Put all the meat, onion and mushrooms back in the pan. Reduce the heat, and stir in the mustard, crème fraîche and cream. Heat through, stir in most of the parsley and season with salt and pepper. Serve with rice or noodles, and scatter over the remaining parsley.

Preparation Time: 10 minutes

Cooking Time: about 20 minutes

Serves: 4

Calories Per Serving: 750

Cook's Tip

Choose bags or bunches of fresh basil, as the larger leaves have a stronger, more peppery flavour than those of plants sold in pots.

Aubergine Parmigiana

2 large aubergines, thinly sliced lengthways

2 tbsp olive oil, plus extra to brush

3 fat garlic cloves, sliced

2 x 200ml tubs fresh napoletana sauce

4 ready-roasted red peppers, roughly chopped

20g (3/4 oz) fresh basil, roughly chopped (see Cook's Tip)

150g (5oz) Taleggio or fontina cheese, coarsely grated

50g (2oz) Parmesan, coarsely grated

salt and ground black pepper

1 Preheat the oven to 200°C (180°C fan oven) mark 6, and preheat the grill until hot. Put the aubergine slices on an oiled baking sheet, brush with olive oil, scatter over the garlic and season with salt and pepper. Grill for 5–6 minutes until golden.

2 Spread a little napoletana sauce over the bottom of an oiled ovenproof dish, then cover with a layer of aubergine and peppers, packing the layers together tightly. Sprinkle a little basil and some of each cheese over the top. Repeat the layers, finishing with a layer of cheese. Season with pepper. Cook in the oven for 20 minutes or until golden. Serve hot.

Preparation Time: 5 minutes

Cooking Time: about 25 minutes

Serves: 4

Calories Per Serving: 370

Cook's Tips

You need coarse-textured good-quality butcher's sausages for this.

To freeze Complete step 3. Add the pasta and cook for 10 minutes – it will continue to cook when you reheat the bolognese. Cool, put in a freezerproof container and freeze for up to three months.

To use Thaw overnight at cool room temperature, put in a pan and add 150ml (¼ pint) water. Bring to the boil, then simmer gently for 10 minutes or until the sauce is hot and the pasta is cooked.

Chunky One-pot Bolognese

3 tbsp olive oil

2 large red onions, finely diced

a few fresh rosemary sprigs

1 large aubergine, finely diced

8 plump coarse sausages

350ml (12fl oz) gutsy red wine

700g (1½lb) passata

4 tbsp sun-dried tomato paste

300ml (½ pint) hot vegetable stock

175g (6oz) small dried pasta such as orecchiette

salt and ground black pepper

1 Heat 2 tbsp of the olive oil in a large, shallow non-stick pan over a low heat. Add the onions and rosemary and cook for 10 minutes or until soft and golden. Add the aubergine and remaining oil and cook over a medium heat for 8–10 minutes until soft and golden.

2 Meanwhile, pull the skin off the sausages and divide each into four rough chunks. Tip the aubergine mixture on to a plate and add the sausage chunks to the hot pan – you won't need any extra oil. Stir the sausage pieces over a high heat for 6–8 minutes until golden and beginning to crisp at the edges.

3 Pour in the wine and leave to bubble for 6–8 minutes until only a little liquid remains. Put the aubergine mixture back in the pan, with the passata, tomato paste and stock.

4 Stir the pasta into the liquid, cover, then simmer for 20 minutes or until the pasta is cooked. Taste and season if needed.

Preparation Time: 10 minutes

Cooking Time: 55 minutes

Serves: 6

Calories Per Serving: 499

Mushroom and Bean Hotpot

3 tbsp olive oil

700g (1½lb) chestnut mushrooms, roughly chopped

1 large onion, finely chopped

2 tbsp plain flour

2 tbsp mild curry paste

150ml (¼ pint) dry white wine

400g can chopped tomatoes

2 tbsp sun-dried tomato paste

2 x 400g cans mixed beans, drained and rinsed

3 tbsp mango chutney

3 tbsp roughly chopped fresh coriander and mint

1 Heat the oil in a large pan over a low heat, and fry the mushrooms and onion until the onion is soft and dark golden. Stir in the flour and curry paste, then cook for 1–2 minutes before adding the wine, tomatoes, tomato paste and beans.

2 Bring to the boil, then simmer gently for 30 minutes or until most of the liquid has reduced. Stir in the chutney and herbs before serving.

Preparation Time: 15 minutes

Cooking Time: 30 minutes

Serves: 6

Calories Per Serving: 280

Freezing Tip

To freeze Complete to the end of step 4, without the garnish. Cool quickly and put in a freezerproof container. Seal and freeze for up to one month.
To use Thaw overnight at cool room temperature. Preheat the oven to 180°C (160°C fan oven) mark 4. Put in a flameproof casserole, and add an extra 150ml (¼ pint) beef stock. Bring to the boil. Cover and reheat for 30 minutes.

Peppered Winter Stew

25g (1oz) plain flour

900g (2lb) stewing venison, beef or lamb, cut into 4cm (1½ in) cubes

5 tbsp oil

225g (8oz) button onions or shallots, peeled with root end intact

225g (8oz) onion, finely chopped

4 garlic cloves, crushed

2 tbsp tomato purée

125ml (4fl oz) red wine vinegar

75cl bottle red wine

2 tbsp redcurrant jelly

1 small bunch of fresh thyme

4 bay leaves

1 tbsp coarsely ground black pepper

6 cloves

900g (2lb) mixed root vegetables, such as carrots, parsnips, turnips and celeriac, cut into 4cm (1½in) chunks; carrots cut a little smaller

600–900ml (1–1½ pints) beef stock

salt and ground black pepper

1 Preheat the oven to 180°C (160°C fan oven) mark 4. Put the flour into a plastic bag, season with salt and pepper, then toss the meat in it.

2 Heat 3 tbsp oil in a large flameproof casserole over a medium heat, and brown the meat well, in small batches. Remove and put to one side.

3 Heat the remaining oil and fry the button onions or shallots for 5 minutes or until golden. Add the chopped onion and the garlic and cook, stirring, until soft and golden. Add the tomato purée and cook for a further 2 minutes, then add the vinegar and wine and bring to the boil. Bubble for 10 minutes.

4 Add the redcurrant jelly, thyme, bay leaves, 1 tbsp pepper, cloves and meat to the pan, together with the vegetables and enough stock to barely cover the meat and vegetables. Bring to the boil, cover and cook in the oven for 1¾–2¼ hours until the meat is very tender. Serve hot.

Preparation Time: 20 minutes

Cooking Time: 2¼ hours

Serves: 6

Calories Per Serving: 540

Freezing Tip

When you have layered the lamb, vegetables, feta, yogurt sauce and Parmesan in the dishes at step 3, cool, wrap and freeze for up to three months.
To use Thaw overnight at cool room temperature. Cook at 190°C (170°C fan oven) mark 5 for 45–50 minutes until piping hot in the centre.

Greek Lamb and Feta Layer

5 tbsp olive oil

1 large onion, finely chopped

900g (2lb) lamb mince

2 garlic cloves, crushed

2 tbsp tomato purée

2 x 400g cans plum tomatoes in tomato juice

3 tbsp Worcestershire sauce

2 tbsp freshly chopped oregano

3 large potatoes, about 1kg (2¼ lb) total weight

2 large aubergines, trimmed and cut into 5mm (¼ in) slices

1kg (2¼ lb) Greek yogurt

4 large eggs

50g (2oz) freshly grated Parmesan

pinch of freshly grated nutmeg

200g (7oz) feta cheese, crumbled

salt and ground black pepper

Preparation Time: 20 minutes

Cooking Time: about 1 hour 50 minutes

Serves: 8

Calories Per Serving: 684

1 Heat 2 tbsp oil in a large pan, add the onion and cook over a low heat for 10 minutes or until soft. Put the mince in a large non-stick frying pan and cook over a high heat, breaking it up with a spoon, until no liquid remains and the lamb is brown, 10–15 minutes. Add the garlic and tomato purée, and cook for 2 minutes. Add the lamb to the onion with the tomatoes, Worcestershire sauce and oregano. Bring to the boil and season with salt and pepper. Simmer for 30–40 minutes until the lamb is tender.

2 Meanwhile, cook the potatoes in boiling salted water for 20–30 minutes until tender, then drain and cool. Peel and slice thickly. Preheat the oven to 180°C (160°C fan oven) mark 4. Brush the aubergine slices with the remaining oil. Preheat two non-stick frying pans and cook the aubergine for 2–3 minutes on each side until soft. Mix together the yogurt, eggs and half the Parmesan, season with nutmeg, salt and pepper.

3 Divide the lamb between two 1.4 litre (2½ pint) ovenproof dishes or eight individual dishes. Layer the potato, feta and aubergine on top. Pour the yogurt sauce over and sprinkle with the remaining Parmesan. Cook for 35–40 minutes until the top has browned and it's piping hot in the centre.

2 medium baking potatoes, thinly sliced

a little freshly grated nutmeg

600ml (1 pint) white sauce (use a
ready-made sauce or make your own)

$\frac{1}{2}$ x 390g can fried onions

250g (9oz) frozen peas

450g (1lb) cooked chicken, shredded

20g pack garlic butter, sliced

a little butter to grease

salt and ground black pepper

Oven-baked Chicken with Garlic Potatoes

1 Preheat the oven to 180°C (160°C fan oven) mark 4. Layer half the potatoes over the base of a 2.4 litre (4¼ pint) shallow ovenproof dish and season with the nutmeg, salt and pepper. Pour the white sauce over and shake the dish, so that the sauce settles through the gaps in the potatoes.

2 Spread half the onions on top, then scatter over half the peas. Arrange the shredded chicken on top, then add the remaining peas and onions. Finish with the remaining potatoes, arranged in an even layer, and dot with garlic butter. Season with salt and pepper.

3 Cover tightly with buttered foil and cook for hour. Turn the heat up to 200°C (180°C fan oven) mark 6, remove the foil and continue to cook for 20–30 minutes until the potatoes are golden and tender.

Preparation Time: 10 minutes

Cooking Time: 1½ hours

Serves: 6

Calories Per Serving: 376

1 tbsp olive oil

1.1kg (2½lb) smoked gammon joint

8 shallots, roughly chopped

3 carrots, cut into chunks

3 celery sticks, cut into chunks

4 large Desirée potatoes, quartered

450ml (15fl oz) apple juice

450ml (15fl oz) hot vegetable stock

½ small Savoy cabbage, shredded

25g (1oz) butter

One-pot Gammon

1 Preheat the oven to 190°C (170°C fan oven) mark 5. Heat the oil in a large flameproof casserole, add the gammon joint and cook, turning once or twice, for 5 minutes until brown all over. Remove from the pan and put to one side.

2 Add the shallots, carrots and celery to the casserole, and fry for 3–4 minutes until starting to soften.

3 Put the gammon back in the casserole with the potatoes, apple juice and stock. Cover and bring to the boil. Transfer to the oven and cook for 50 minutes until the meat is cooked through and the vegetables are tender.

4 Put the casserole back on the hob over a low heat, and stir in the cabbage. Simmer for 2–3 minutes, then stir in the butter and serve immediately.

Preparation Time: 15 minutes

Cooking Time: 1 hour 10 minutes

Serves: 4

Calories Per Serving: 698

Try Something Different

Instead of paprika, use 1 tsp each ground cumin and ground coriander. Garnish with freshly chopped coriander.

Spiced Bean and Vegetable Stew

3 tbsp olive oil

2 small onions, sliced

2 garlic cloves, crushed

1 tbsp sweet paprika

1 small dried red chilli, seeded and finely chopped (see page 14)

700g (1½lb) sweet potatoes, peeled and cubed

700g (1½lb) pumpkin, peeled and cut into chunks

125g (4oz) okra, trimmed

500g jar passata

400g can haricot or cannellini beans, drained

salt and ground black pepper

1 Heat the oil in a large heavy-based pan over a very gentle heat. Add the onions and garlic, and cook for 5 minutes.

2 Stir in the paprika and chilli, and cook for 2 minutes, then add the sweet potatoes, pumpkin, okra, passata and 900ml (1½ pints) cold water. Season well with salt and pepper.

3 Cover the pan, bring to the boil and simmer for 20 minutes until the vegetables are tender. Add the beans, cook for 3 minutes to warm through, then serve.

Preparation Time: 15 minutes

Cooking Time: 35 minutes

Serves: 6

Calories Per Serving: 262

Try Something Different

Use pork escalopes cut into thin strips instead of chicken.

1 tbsp sunflower oil

350g (12oz) skinless chicken breast fillets, cut into strips

1 garlic clove, crushed

300–350g tub or jar curry sauce

400g can aduki beans, drained and rinsed

175g (6oz) ready-to-eat dried apricots

150g (5oz) natural bio yogurt

125g (4oz) ready-to-eat baby spinach

Chicken, Bean and Spinach Curry

1 Heat the oil in a large pan over a medium heat, and fry the chicken strips with the garlic until golden. Add the curry sauce, beans and apricots, then cover and simmer gently for 15 minutes or until the chicken is tender.

2 Over a low heat, stir in half the yogurt, keeping the curry hot without boiling it, then stir in the spinach until it just begins to wilt. Serve immediately, with a spoonful of yogurt.

Preparation Time: 10 minutes

Cooking Time: about 20 minutes

Serves: 4

Calories Per Serving: 364

Cook's Tip

Check the ingredients in the Thai curry paste: some contain shrimp and are therefore not suitable for vegetarians.

250g (9oz) fresh tofu

2 tbsp light soy sauce

½ red chilli, chopped (see page 14)

5cm (2in) piece fresh root ginger, peeled and grated

1 tbsp olive oil

1 onion, finely sliced

2 tbsp Thai red curry paste

200ml (7fl oz) coconut milk

900ml (1½ pints) hot vegetable stock

200g (7oz) baby sweetcorn, halved lengthways

200g (7oz) fine green beans

250g (9oz) medium rice noodles

salt and ground black pepper

2 spring onions, sliced diagonally, and 2 tbsp freshly chopped coriander to garnish

1 lime, cut into wedges, to serve

Tofu Noodle Curry

1 Drain the tofu, pat it dry and cut it into large cubes. Put the tofu in a shallow dish with the soy sauce, chilli and ginger. Toss to coat, then leave to marinate for 30 minutes.

2 Heat the oil in a large pan over a medium heat, add the onion and fry for 10 minutes, stirring, until golden. Add the curry paste and cook for 2 minutes.

3 Add the tofu and marinade, coconut milk, stock and sweetcorn, and season with salt and pepper. Bring to the boil, add the green beans, then reduce the heat and simmer for 8–10 minutes.

4 Meanwhile, put the noodles in a large bowl, pour boiling water over them and soak for 30 seconds. Drain the noodles, then stir into the curry. Pour into bowls and garnish with the spring onions and coriander. Serve immediately, with lime wedges.

Preparation Time: 15 minutes, plus 30 minutes marinating

Cooking Time: about 25 minutes

Serves: 4

Calories Per Serving: 367

Try Something Different

Replace the apricots with ready-to-eat prunes.

2 tbsp olive oil

4 chicken thighs

1 onion, chopped

2 tsp cinnamon

2 tbsp honey

150g (5oz) ready-to-eat dried apricots

75g (3oz) blanched almonds

250ml (9fl oz) hot chicken stock

salt and ground black pepper

freshly chopped flat-leafed parsley to garnish

couscous to serve

Chicken Tagine with Apricots

1　Heat 1 tbsp oil in a large flameproof casserole. Add the chicken thighs and fry for 5 minutes or until brown. Remove from the casserole, set aside and keep warm.

2　Add the onion to the pan with the remaining oil and fry for 10 minutes until softened. Return the chicken to the pan with the cinnamon, honey, apricots, almonds and stock. Season well with salt and pepper, stir once, then cover and bring to the boil. Simmer for 45 minutes or until the chicken is falling off the bone.

3　Garnish with chopped parsley and serve with couscous.

Preparation Time: 5 minutes

Cooking Time: 1 hour

Serves: 4

Calories Per Serving: 500

Cook's Tip

Italian Dolcelatte cheese has a much milder flavour than Stilton or Roquefort; it also has a deliciously rich, creamy texture.

Spinach and Cheese Lasagne

125g (4oz) fresh or frozen leaf spinach, thawed

40g (1½oz) fresh basil, roughly chopped

250g (9oz) ricotta cheese

5 pieces marinated artichokes, drained and chopped

350g carton cheese sauce

175g (6oz) Dolcelatte cheese, roughly diced

9 sheets fresh egg lasagne

25g (1oz) pinenuts, toasted

1 Preheat the oven to 180°C (160°C fan oven) mark 4. Chop the spinach finely (if it was frozen, squeeze out the excess liquid first). Put in a bowl with the basil, ricotta cheese, artichokes and 6 tbsp cheese sauce. Mix well.

2 Beat the Dolcelatte into the remaining cheese sauce. Layer the ricotta mixture, lasagne, then cheese sauce into a 23 x 23cm (9 x 9in) ovenproof dish. Repeat, finishing with cheese sauce.

3 Cook the lasagne for 40 minutes. Sprinkle over the pinenuts and put back in the oven for a further 10–15 minutes until golden.

Preparation Time: 30 minutes

Cooking Time: 50–55 minutes

Serves: 6

Calories Per Serving: 442

4 cloves

1 tsp each coriander seeds and cumin seeds

seeds from 3 cardamom pods

2 garlic cloves, roughly chopped

2.5cm (1in) piece fresh root ginger, peeled and roughly chopped

1 small onion, roughly chopped

2 tbsp sunflower oil

1 tbsp sesame oil

1 tbsp Thai red curry paste

1 tsp turmeric

450g (1lb) sirloin steak, cut into 3cm (1¼ in) cubes

225g (8oz) potatoes, quartered

4 tomatoes, quartered

1 tsp sugar

1 tbsp light soy sauce

300ml (½ pint) coconut milk

150ml (¼ pint) beef stock

4 small red chillies, bruised (see page 14)

50g (2oz) cashew nuts

rice and stir-fried green vegetables to serve

Preparation Time: 20 minutes, plus cooling

Cooking Time: about 30 minutes

Serves: 4

Calories Per Serving: 443

Thai Beef Curry

1 Put the cloves, coriander, cumin and cardamom seeds in a small heavy-based frying pan and fry over a high heat for 1–2 minutes until the spices release their aroma. Be careful that they do not burn. Leave to cool slightly, then grind to a powder in a spice grinder or blender.

2 Put the garlic, ginger and onion in a blender or food processor and whiz to form a smooth paste. Heat the sunflower and sesame oils in a wok or deep frying pan. Add the onion purée and the curry paste and stir-fry for 5 minutes, then add the ground roasted spices and turmeric and fry for a further 5 minutes.

3 Add the beef to the pan and fry for 5 minutes until browned on all sides. Add the potatoes, tomatoes, sugar, soy sauce, coconut milk, stock and chillies to the pan. Bring to the boil, then lower the heat, cover and simmer gently for about 15 minutes or until the beef is tender and the potatoes are cooked.

4 Stir in the cashew nuts and serve the curry with rice and stir-fried vegetables.

Cook's Tip

Oil-water spray is far lower in calories than oil alone and, as it sprays on thinly and evenly, you'll use less. Fill one-eighth of a travel-size spray bottle with oil such as sunflower, light olive or vegetable (rapeseed) oil, then top up with water. To use, shake well before spraying.

oil-water spray (see Cook's Tip)

2 red onions, chopped

1½ tsp each ground coriander and ground cumin

½ tsp ground paprika

2 garlic cloves, crushed

2 sun-dried tomatoes, chopped

¼ tsp crushed dried chilli flakes

125ml (4fl oz) red wine

300ml (½ pint) vegetable stock

2 x 400g cans brown or green lentils, drained and rinsed

2 x 400g cans chopped tomatoes

salt and ground black pepper

sugar to taste

Lentil Chilli

1 Spray a saucepan with the oil-water spray and cook the onions for 5 minutes until softened. Add the coriander, cumin and paprika. Combine the garlic, sun-dried tomatoes, chilli, wine and stock and add to the pan. Cover and simmer for 5–7 minutes. Uncover and simmer until the onions are very tender and the liquid is almost gone.

2 Stir in the lentils and canned tomatoes and season with salt and pepper. Simmer, uncovered, for 15 minutes until thick. Stir in the sugar to taste. Remove from the heat.

3 Ladle out a quarter of the mixture and whiz in a food processor or blender. Combine the puréed and unpuréed portions and serve.

Preparation Time: 10 minutes

Cooking Time: 30 minutes

Serves: 6

Calories Per Serving: 191

Cook's Tip

Choose aubergines that are firm, shiny and blemish-free, with a bright green stem.

Aubergine and Lentil Curry

3 tbsp olive oil

2 aubergines, cut into 2.5cm (1in) chunks

1 onion, chopped

2 tbsp mild curry paste

3 x 400g cans chopped tomatoes

200ml (7fl oz) hot vegetable stock

150g (5oz) red lentils, rinsed

100g (3½oz) spinach leaves

25g (1oz) fresh coriander, roughly chopped, plus extra leaves to garnish

2 tbsp fat-free Greek yogurt

rice to serve

1 Heat 2 tbsp of the oil in a large pan over a low heat, and fry the aubergine chunks until golden. Remove from the pan and put to one side.

2 Heat the remaining oil in the same pan, and fry the onion for 8–10 minutes until soft. Add the curry paste and stir-fry for a further 2 minutes.

3 Add the tomatoes, stock, lentils and fried aubergines to the pan. Bring to the boil, then reduce the heat to a low simmer, half-cover with a lid and simmer for 25 minutes or according to the lentils' packet instructions.

4 At the end of the cooking time, stir the spinach, coriander and yogurt through the curry. Serve with rice and scatter over the coriander leaves.

Preparation Time: 10 minutes

Cooking Time: 40–45 minutes

Serves: 4

Calories Per Serving: 335

Cook's Tip

If you can't find half-fat coconut milk, use half a can of full-fat coconut milk and make up the difference with water or stock. Freeze the remaining milk for up to one month.

Thai Red Seafood Curry

1 tbsp vegetable oil

3 tbsp Thai red curry paste

450g (1lb) monkfish tail, boned to make 350g (12oz) fillet, sliced into rounds

350g (12oz) large raw peeled prawns, deveined

400ml can half-fat coconut milk

200ml (7fl oz) fish stock

juice of 1 lime

1–2 tbsp Thai fish sauce

125g (4oz) mangetouts

3 tbsp fresh coriander, roughly torn

salt and ground black pepper

1 Heat the oil in a wok or large non-stick frying pan. Add the curry paste and cook for 1–2 minutes.

2 Add the monkfish and prawns and stir well to coat in the curry paste. Add the coconut milk, stock, lime juice and fish sauce. Stir all the ingredients together and bring just to the boil.

3 Add the mangetouts and simmer for 5 minutes or until the mangetouts and fish are tender. Stir in the coriander and check the seasoning, adding salt and pepper to taste. Serve immediately.

Preparation Time: 15 minutes

Cooking Time: 8–10 minutes

Serves: 4

Calories Per Serving: 252

Puddings

Spiced Winter Fruit

Rich Chocolate Pots

Bread and Butter Pudding

Oranges with Caramel Sauce

Toffee Cheesecake

Rhubarb and Pear Crumble

Figs in Cinnamon Syrup

Rice Pudding

Sticky Maple Syrup Pineapple

Orange Eggy Bread

Quick Apple Tart

Golden Honey Fruits

Apple and Blueberry Strudel

Cinnamon Pancakes

Chocolate Cherry Roll

Apples with Butterscotch Sauce

Baked Orange Custard

Freezing Tip

Put the fruit and syrup into a freezerproof container, leave to cool, then cover with a tight-fitting lid and freeze for up to three months.
To use Thaw overnight in the refrigerator and serve cold.

150ml (¼ pint) port

150ml (¼ pint) freshly squeezed orange juice

75g (3oz) soft light brown sugar

1 cinnamon stick

6 whole cardamom pods, lightly crushed

5cm (2in) piece fresh root ginger, peeled and thinly sliced

50g (2oz) large muscatel raisins or dried blueberries

1 small pineapple, peeled, core removed and thinly sliced

1 mango, peeled, stoned and thickly sliced

3 tangerines, peeled and halved horizontally

3 fresh figs, halved

Spiced Winter Fruit

1 First, make the syrup. Pour the port and orange juice into a small pan, then add the sugar and 300ml (½ pint) cold water. Bring to the boil, stirring all the time. Add the cinnamon stick, cardamom pods and ginger, then bubble gently for 15 minutes.

2 Put all the fruit in a serving bowl. Remove the cinnamon stick and cardamom pods from the syrup – or leave in for a spicier flavour – then pour over the fruit. Leave to cool, and serve cold.

Preparation Time: 20 minutes

Cooking Time: 20 minutes, plus cooling

Serves: 6

Calories Per Serving: 207

Get Ahead

Make the chocolate curls and keep in a sealed container in the refrigerator for up to one day.

300g bar chocolate-flavour cake covering

300g (11oz) plain chocolate (at least 70% cocoa solids), broken into chunks

300ml (½ pint) double cream

250g (9oz) mascarpone

3 tbsp Cognac

1 tbsp vanilla extract

6 tbsp crème fraîche

Rich Chocolate Pots

1 Put the cake covering on a board and, using a very sharp knife, scrape against it to make 12 curls. (Use a vegetable peeler if you find it easier.) Chill until needed.

2 Melt the plain chocolate in a heatproof bowl over a pan of gently simmering water, making sure the base of the bowl doesn't touch the water. Remove from the heat and add the cream, mascarpone, Cognac and vanilla. Mix well – the hot chocolate will melt into the cream and mascarpone.

3 Divide the mixture among six 150ml (¼ pint) glasses, and chill for 20 minutes. Spoon some crème fraîche on top of each chocolate pot, and decorate with the chocolate curls.

Preparation Time: 10 minutes, plus 20 minutes chilling

Cooking Time: 10 minutes

Serves: 6

Calories Per Serving: 895

Bread and Butter Pudding

400g (14oz) panettone, cut into 1cm (½ in) slices, then diagonally in half again to make triangles

4 medium eggs

450ml (¾ pint) milk

3 tbsp golden icing sugar

1 Preheat the oven to 180°C (160°C fan oven) mark 4. Arrange the slices of panettone in four 300ml (½ pint) gratin dishes or one 1.1 litre (2 pint) dish.

2 Beat the eggs, milk and 2 tbsp of the sugar in a bowl, and pour over the panettone. Soak for 10 minutes.

3 Put the pudding(s) in the oven, and bake for 30–40 minutes. Dust with the remaining icing sugar to serve.

Preparation Time: 10 minutes, plus 10 minutes soaking

Cooking Time: 30–40 minutes

Serves: 6

Calories Per Serving: 450

Cook's Tip

Use thick-skinned oranges, such as navel oranges, as they're the easiest to peel.

Oranges with Caramel Sauce

6 oranges

25g (1oz) butter

2 tbsp golden caster sugar

2 tbsp Grand Marnier

2 tbsp marmalade

grated zest and juice of 1 large orange

1 Preheat the oven to 200°C (180°C fan oven) mark 6. Cut away the peel and pith from the oranges, then put the oranges into a roasting tin just big enough to hold them.

2 Melt the butter in a pan and add the sugar, Grand Marnier, marmalade, orange zest and juice. Heat gently to dissolve the sugar.

3 Pour the sauce over the oranges, and bake in the oven for 30–40 minutes.

Preparation Time: 15 minutes

Cooking Time: 30–40 minutes

Serves: 6

Calories Per Serving: 139

Cook's Tip

To slice the cheesecake easily, use a sharp knife dipped into a jug of boiling water and then wiped dry. **If your toffee sauce is too thick** to drizzle, put it into a microwave-safe bowl and heat on medium power for 10–20 seconds.

300g (11oz) digestive biscuits, broken

125g (4oz) butter, melted

For the filling

450g (1lb) curd cheese

150ml (¼ pint) double cream

juice of ½ lemon

3 medium eggs, beaten

50g (2oz) golden caster sugar

6 tbsp dulce de leche toffee sauce, plus extra to drizzle

Toffee Cheesecake

1 Preheat the oven to 200°C (180°C fan oven) mark 6. To make the crust, put the biscuits into a food processor and grind until fine. (Alternatively, put them in a plastic bag and crush with a rolling pin. Transfer to a bowl.) Add the butter and blend briefly, or stir in, to combine. Press the mixture evenly into the base and up the sides of a 20.5cm (8in) springform cake tin. Chill in the refrigerator.

2 To make the filling, put the curd cheese and cream in a food processor or blender and blend until smooth. Add the lemon juice, eggs, sugar and toffee sauce, then blend again until smooth. Pour into the biscuit case and bake for 10 minutes. Reduce the oven temperature to 180°C (160°C fan oven) mark 4, then bake for 45 minutes or until set and golden brown.

3 Turn off the oven, leave the door ajar and let the cheesecake cool. When completely cool, chill to firm up the crust.

4 Remove the cheesecake from the tin by running a knife around the edge. Open the tin carefully, then use a palette knife to ease the cheesecake out. Cut into wedges, put on a serving plate, then drizzle with toffee sauce.

Preparation Time: 15 minutes, plus chilling

Cooking Time: 55 minutes–1 hour

Serves: 10

Calories Per Serving: 439

450g (1lb) rhubarb, cut into 2.5cm (1in) pieces

2 ripe pears, peeled, cored and roughly chopped

75g (3oz) demerara sugar

1 tsp ground cinnamon

50g (2oz) butter, chilled

75g (3oz) self-raising flour

2 shortbread fingers

50g (2oz) hazelnuts

Greek yogurt to serve

Rhubarb and Pear Crumble

1 Preheat the oven to 180°C (160°C fan oven) mark 4. Put the fruit into a small shallow baking dish and sprinkle over 25g (1oz) sugar and the cinnamon. Mix together well.

2 Next, make the crumble mixture. Put the butter in a food processor, add the flour and the remaining sugar and whiz until it looks like rough breadcrumbs. Alternatively, rub the fat into the flour by hand or using a pastry cutter, then stir in the sugar.

3 Break the shortbread fingers into pieces and add to the processor with the hazelnuts. Whiz for 4–5 seconds until the crumble is blended but still looks rough. Alternatively, crush the shortbread with a rolling pin and chop the hazelnuts, then stir into the crumble. Sprinkle the crumble over the fruit, spreading it up to the edges and pressing down with the back of a wooden spoon.

4 Bake for 40–45 minutes until the topping is golden brown and crisp. Serve with yogurt.

Preparation Time:	25 minutes
Cooking Time:	40–45 minutes
Serves:	6
Calories Per Serving:	255

Figs in Cinnamon Syrup

1 orange

1 lemon

300ml (½ pint) red wine

50g (2oz) golden caster sugar

1 cinnamon stick

450g (1lb) ready-to-eat dried figs

mascarpone cheese or ice cream to serve

1 Pare the zest from the orange and the lemon, and put in a medium pan. Squeeze the orange and the lemon and add their juice, the wine, sugar and cinnamon stick to the pan. Bring very slowly to the boil, stirring occasionally.

2 Add the figs. Simmer very gently for 20 minutes until plump and soft. Remove the figs, zest and cinnamon with a slotted spoon, and transfer to a serving bowl.

3 Bring the liquid to the boil once again, and bubble for about 5 minutes until syrupy. Pour over the figs, then cool, cover and chill.

4 If you like, warm the figs in the syrup for 3–4 minutes, then serve with the mascarpone cheese or ice cream.

Preparation Time: 15 minutes

Cooking Time: 35 minutes, plus cooling and chilling

Serves: 4

Calories Per Serving: 336

Rice Pudding

125g (4oz) short-grain pudding rice

1.1 litres (2 pints) full-fat milk

4 tbsp golden caster sugar

grated zest of 1 small orange

2 tsp vanilla extract

whole nutmeg to grate

1 Preheat the oven to 180°C (160°C fan oven) mark 4. Lightly butter a 900ml (1½ pint) ovenproof dish. Add the rice, milk, sugar, orange zest and vanilla extract, and stir everything together. Grate a little nutmeg all over the top of the mixture.

2 Bake the pudding for 1½ hours or until the top is golden brown, then serve.

Preparation Time: 5 minutes

Cooking Time: 1½ hours

Serves: 6

Calories Per Serving: 235

Sticky Maple Syrup Pineapple

1 large fresh pineapple

200ml (7fl oz) maple syrup

1 Peel the pineapple and cut lengthways into quarters. Cut away the central woody core from each pineapple quarter. Slice each one lengthways into four to make 16 wedges.

2 Pour the maple syrup into a large non-stick frying pan and heat for 2 minutes. Add the pineapple and fry for 3 minutes, turning once, until warmed through.

3 Divide the pineapple among four serving plates, drizzle the maple syrup over and around the pineapple, and serve immediately.

Preparation Time: 15 minutes

Cooking Time: 5 minutes

Serves: 4

Calories Per Serving: 231

2 large eggs

150ml (¼ pint) milk

finely grated zest of 1 orange

50g (2oz) butter

8 slices raisin bread, halved diagonally

1 tbsp caster sugar

vanilla ice cream and orange segments to serve (optional)

Orange Eggy Bread

1 Lightly whisk the eggs, milk and orange zest together in a bowl.

2 Heat the butter in a large frying pan over a medium heat. Dip the slices of raisin bread into the egg mixture, and fry on both sides until golden.

3 Sprinkle the bread with the sugar, and serve immediately with ice cream and orange slices if you like.

Preparation Time: 10 minutes

Cooking Time: 15 minutes

Serves: 4

Calories Per Serving: 358

Quick Apple Tart

375g packet all-butter ready-rolled puff pastry

500g (1lb 2oz) Cox's apples, cored, thinly sliced and tossed in the juice of 1 lemon

golden icing sugar to dust

1 Preheat the oven to 200°C (180°C fan oven) mark 6. Put the pastry on a 28 x 38cm (11 x 15in) baking sheet, and roll lightly with a rolling pin to smooth down the pastry. Score lightly around the edge, to create a 3cm (1¼ in) border.

2 Put the apple slices on top of the pastry, within the border. Turn the edge of the pastry halfway over, so that it reaches the edge of the apples, then press down and use your fingers to crimp the edge. Dust heavily with icing sugar.

3 Bake in the oven for 20–25 minutes until the pastry is cooked and the sugar has caramelised. Serve warm, dusted with more icing sugar.

Preparation Time: 10 minutes

Cooking Time: 20–25 minutes

Serves: 8

Calories Per Serving: 221

Golden Honey Fruits

900g (2lb) selection of tropical fruit, such as pineapple, mango, papaya and banana

3 tbsp clear honey

Greek yogurt to serve

mixed spice to sprinkle

1 Preheat the grill to high. Peel the fruit as necessary, and cut into wedges.

2 Put the fruit on a foil-lined grill pan, drizzle with the honey and cook under the grill for 5–8 minutes until caramelised.

3 Serve with the yogurt, sprinkled with a little mixed spice.

Preparation Time: 5 minutes

Cooking Time: 5–8 minutes

Serves: 4

Calories Per Serving: 160

700g (1½ lb) red apples, quartered, cored and thickly sliced

1 tbsp lemon juice

2 tbsp golden caster sugar

100g (3½ oz) dried blueberries

1 tbsp olive oil

6 sheets of filo pastry, thawed if frozen

Apple and Blueberry Strudel

1 Preheat the oven to 190°C (170°C fan oven) mark 5. Put the apples into a bowl and mix with the lemon juice, 1 tbsp sugar and the blueberries.

2 Warm the olive oil. Lay three sheets of filo pastry side by side, overlapping the long edges. Brush with the oil. Cover with three more sheets of filo and brush again.

3 Tip the apple mixture on to the pastry and roll up from a long edge. Put on to a non-stick baking sheet. Brush with the remaining oil and sprinkle with the remaining caster sugar. Bake for 40 minutes or until the pastry is golden and the apples soft. Serve warm.

Preparation Time: 15 minutes

Cooking Time: 40 minutes

Serves: 6

Calories Per Serving: 178

Try Something Different

Serve with sliced bananas and vanilla ice cream
instead of the fruit compote and yogurt.

150g (5oz) plain flour

½ tsp ground cinnamon

1 medium egg

300ml (½ pint) skimmed milk

olive oil to fry

fruit compote or sugar and Greek yogurt to serve

Cinnamon Pancakes

1 In a large bowl, whisk together the flour, cinnamon, egg and milk to make a smooth batter. Leave to stand for 20 minutes.

2 Heat a heavy-based frying pan over a medium heat. When the pan is really hot, add 1 tsp oil, pour in a ladleful of batter and tilt the pan to coat the base with an even layer. Cook for 1 minute or until golden. Flip over and cook for 1 minute, then turn out and keep warm. Repeat with the remaining batter, adding more oil if necessary, to make six pancakes. Serve with a fruit compote or a sprinkling of sugar, and a dollop of yogurt.

Preparation Time: 5 minutes

Cooking Time: 20 minutes

Serves: 6

Calories Per Serving: 141

Try Something Different

Raspberries make a great alternative to cherries: use 350g (12oz) fresh raspberries and 1 tbsp raspberry jam.

Chocolate Cherry Roll

4 tbsp cocoa

100ml (3½fl oz) milk, plus 3 tbsp

5 medium eggs, separated

125g (4oz) golden caster sugar

400g can pitted cherries

1–2 tbsp cherry jam

cocoa and icing sugar to dust

1 Preheat the oven to 180°C (160°C fan oven) mark 4 and line a 30.5 x 20.5cm (12 x 8in) Swiss-roll tin with baking parchment. Mix the cocoa and 3 tbsp milk in a bowl. Heat 100ml (3½fl oz) milk in a pan until almost boiling. Add to the bowl, stirring. Cool for 10 minutes.

2 Whisk the egg whites in a clean grease-free bowl until soft peaks form. Whisk together the egg yolks and sugar until pale and thick, then gradually whisk in the cooled milk. Fold in the egg whites. Spoon into the prepared tin and level the surface. Bake for 25 minutes or until just firm.

3 Turn out on to a board lined with baking parchment and leave to cool for 5 minutes, then loosely roll up and leave until cold. Unroll. Drain the cherries and chop them. Spread the jam over the roulade and top with the cherries. Roll up from the shortest end. Dust with cocoa and icing sugar, cut into slices and serve.

Preparation Time: 15 minutes

Cooking Time: 25–30 minutes, plus cooling

Serves: 8

Calories Per Serving: 180

Get Ahead

Complete step 1 up to 4 hours in advance.
Make the sauce (step 3), then cool, cover and chill for up to one day.
To use Complete the recipe and bring the sauce back to the boil to serve.

Apples with Butterscotch Sauce

125g (4oz) sultanas

2 tbsp brandy

6 large Bramley apples, cored

4 tbsp soft brown sugar

2 tbsp apple juice

125g (4oz) hazelnuts, chopped and toasted

ricotta cheese to serve

For the butterscotch sauce

125g (4oz) butter

125g (4oz) soft brown sugar

2 tbsp golden syrup

2 tbsp black treacle

4 tbsp brandy

300ml (½ pint) double cream

1 Soak the sultanas in the brandy and set aside for 10 minutes, then stuff each apple with equal amounts.

2 Preheat the oven to 220°C (200°C fan oven) mark 7. Put the apples in a roasting tin, sprinkle over the brown sugar and apple juice. Bake for 15–20 minutes until soft.

3 Meanwhile, make the sauce. Melt the butter, brown sugar, golden syrup and treacle in a heavy-based pan, stirring continuously. When the sugar has dissolved and the mixture is bubbling, stir in the brandy and cream. Bring back to the boil and set aside.

4 Remove the apples from the oven. Serve the apples with the butterscotch sauce, hazelnuts and a dollop of ricotta cheese.

Preparation Time: 5 minutes, plus 10 minutes soaking

Cooking Time: 15–20 minutes

Serves: 6

Calories Per Serving: 821

Cook's Tips

Look for a mild flower honey such as lavender or orange blossom; a strong honey will be overpowering.

The honey needs to be cooked to a golden-brown caramel – any darker and it will become bitter.

The custard may still be wobbly after cooking, but don't worry, it firms up on cooling and chilling.

Baked Orange Custard

grated zest of 1 orange

450ml (³/₄ pint) milk

150ml (¹/₄ pint) double cream

75g (3oz) clear honey (see Cook's Tips)

2 large eggs, plus 4 large yolks

25g (1oz) caster sugar

slivers of orange zest to decorate

1 Put the orange zest, milk and cream in a pan, then bring to the boil. Set aside for 30 minutes to infuse.

2 Preheat the oven to 150°C (130°C fan oven) mark 2. Warm a 1.7 litre (3 pint) soufflé dish or six 150ml (¹/₄ pint) coffee cups in the oven. Bring the honey to the boil in a small heavy-based pan. Bubble for 2–3 minutes until it begins to caramelise (see Cook's Tips). Pour the caramel into the warmed dish or cups and rotate to coat the base. Set aside to cool and harden.

3 Put the eggs, yolks and sugar into a bowl and beat together until smooth. Add the infused milk mixture, stir until well combined, then strain into the dish(es). Put the dish or cups in a roasting tin, and add enough hot water to come halfway up the side(s). Bake for 1 hour 10 minutes for the soufflé dish or 45–50 minutes for the coffee cups until just set in the middle (see Cook's Tips). Leave to cool, then chill for at least 6 hours or overnight. Decorate with orange zest.

Preparation Time: 10 minutes, plus 30 minutes infusing and 15 minutes cooling

Cooking Time: 50 minutes or 1 hour 10 minutes, plus minimum 6 hours chilling

Serves: 6

Calories Per Serving: 268

First published in Great Britain in 2008
by Collins & Brown
10 Southcombe Street
London W14 0RA

An imprint of
Anova Books Company Ltd

Copyright © The National Magazine
Company Limited
and Collins & Brown 2008

The recipes in this volume have been
selected from Good Housekeeping's
Easy To Make series. For more titles in
this series see the back of this book.

The Good Housekeeping website is
www.goodhousekeeping.co.uk

10 9 8 7 6 5 4 3 2 1

ISSN 5022163000111

Reproduction by Dot Gradations Ltd
Printed and bound by Craft Print
International Ltd, Singapore

www.anovabooks.com